War Paint

War Paint

BLACKFOOT AND SARCEE PAINTED BUFFALO ROBES
IN THE ROYAL ONTARIO MUSEUM

ARNI BROWNSTONE

RŌM
ROYAL ONTARIO MUSEUM

First published in 1993 by the Royal Ontario Museum
100 Queen's Park, Toronto, Ontario M5S 2C6

Canadian Cataloguing in Publication Data

Brownstone, Arni, 1947–
    War Paint: Blackfoot and Sarcee painted buffalo
robes in the Royal Ontario Museum

ISBN 0-88854-408-1

1. Siksika Indians - Costume and adornment.   2. Sarsi
Indians - Costume and adornment.   3. Siksika Indians -
Painting.   4. Sarsi Indians - Painting.   5. Siksika
Indians - Wars.   6. Sarsi Indians - Wars.
7. Indians of North America - Costume and Adornment.
8. Indians of North America - Painting.   9. Indians
of North America - Wars.   I. Royal Ontario Museum.
II. Title.

E99.S54B76 1993   970.00497   C93-094138-1

Front cover illustration: Detail from the robe of Sarcee chief Bull Head. Painted in 1908.

Printed and bound in Canada by Friesen Printers

CONTENTS

ILLUSTRATIONS

FOREWORD

During the 19th century the Blackfoot were considered to be one of the most warlike nations in North America. In 1841, Sir George Simpson (Governor of the Hudson's Bay Company from 1821 to 1860) wrote about their raiding expeditions: "By means of their war parties, the fame and fear of the terrible Blackfeet have been extended far and wide throughout the whole of central and Western North America." As late as World War Two the ancient Blackfoot saying, "It is better for a man to be killed in battle than to die of old age or sickness," remained in common use.

The introduction of horses and guns in the early 18th century into Plains Indian culture intensified tribal conflicts. War with its associated ceremonies became an important facet of Plains culture and acted as a powerful unifying force within the tribal organization. By the 19th century the Blackfoot had a well-defined warrior personality. But Blackfoot warfare did not have as its goal the extermination of enemy tribes or the acquisition of their territory. War parties consisted of loosely and hastily organized groups of young men who banded together to capture horses from enemy tribes. These small raiding parties were disbanded immediately after their return home. The killing or scalping of an enemy ranked very low in their value system. War honours were based more on personal bravery, the highest honour being that of counting a coup (touching an enemy in battle). Warriors were motivated by a desire for recognition of their bravery and for personal gain, that is, for the wealth and status that ownership of a large number of horses would confer upon them. This kind of war-

fare, as much as the buffalo hunt, was an integral part of the economy and ethos of Blackfoot culture.

The warrior ethic began at birth and continued throughout life. When a male child was born he was given a name that remained with him until his teenage years; then he was expected to go to war to earn a man's name. When naming a female child, the tribal name-giver often drew upon his own war exploits; it was not uncommon for a woman to have a name such as Good Killer, Double Gun Woman, or Counting Coups on Both Sides.

Blackfoot children were brought up to view war as an opportunity for men to acquire status and riches. The games played by boys during the pre-teenage period usually had some connection to war. In the evenings, boys were told tales that extolled the virtues of warrior heroes. They were taught aphorisms such as "Be brave and cunning in war"; "Fear not death, none but cowards fear to die"; and "Revenge yourself on your enemies."

The exploits of warriors were recorded as pictographs on robes, on tipis, and in rock paintings. Men's and women's clothing designs or decorations were sometimes influenced by war experiences. Certain types of men's shirts were cut and slashed to represent arrow and lance cuts; costumes were painted with war-related designs and decorated with scalp-locks taken in battle.

Religious practices in Blackfoot culture were often related to war. If a warrior had a vision, he might be "given" an object by his spirit protector and be instructed to paint his face or wear his hair in a certain fashion. For example, one Blood chief, Red Crow, was told to wear a blade of grass in his hair so that he would never be injured in battle.

While fur traders, missionaries, policemen, soldiers, and Indian agents, bringing in their wake thousands upon thousands of white settlers, had an obvious and significant impact on Plains Indian society, the loss of the buffalo was a crushing blow. By the late 1870s the once seemingly endless numbers of buffalo on the prairies had virtually disappeared. With their main food staple gone, the Indians had little choice but to settle onto the reserve lands. It was here that the Indian agents, the police, and the missionaries carried out the government's "civilization" policy, with mixed success. Some aspects of Christianity were incorporated into the warrior ethic, for example, one of the Blackfoot "Eleven Commandments" of 1896 stated that one should kill only one's enemies. The old lifestyle of the warrior continued through the late 19th and into the 20th century. Young men on the Blood Reserve rode south to raid the Gros Ventres in Montana in 1887 and the Crow in 1889. In 1905 seven Bloods were caught stealing horses from the Mormons; they had been running the horses over into the Kootenay River area in British Columbia where they were selling them to a local rancher.

Despite the efforts of the missionary teachers and the Indian agents, traditional culture, and in particular the warrior ethic, survived among the Blackfoot. The advent of World War One in 1914 offered a new opportunity for expression of the warrior ethic. According to Treaty No. 3 (1873), natives were exempt from fighting in Canada's wars. During the treaty negotiations, one of the chiefs had said, "If you should get into trouble with the nations, I do not wish to walk out and expose my young men to aid you in any of your wars." Alexander Morris, the government negotiator, had replied that "the English never call the Indians out of their country to fight their battles."

So why did the Indians, many Blackfoot among them, choose to enlist? Many western Indians had a close association with the Crown—it was with this "person" that the treaties had been made. Also, the war no doubt offered them an escape from the stagnation of reserve life. But perhaps the main reason was that young Indian men saw their chance to become warriors and to experience the exhilaration and achieve the honours that they had only heard about from their fathers and grandfathers. Indians returning from the War were treated as heroes and received all the honours that had traditionally been accorded to brave warriors. In 1919, the Bloods held a victory Sun Dance for all the returning veterans of World War One. Similarly, following World War Two, during the organization of the Union of Saskatchewan Indians in 1946, many of the members were war veterans whose war exploits gave them the right to be heard at this political function. One among them, William Bird, began his speech by stating, "I happen to be a veteran of both of the great wars."

Set forth in this book are the war histories of eight veteran chiefs of the Plains, members of the last generation of nomadic Blackfoot and Sarcee. Their exploits were painted in pictographic form on buffalo robes and subsequently translated into English from the warriors' own narrations. In reproducing both their pictures and their words, *War Paint* provides a valuable record of the past and illuminates a vital aspect of Plains Indian culture.

James Dempsey
Director
School of Native Studies
University of Alberta

ACKNOWLEDGMENTS

This study would not have been possible without the work of Mary Fitz-Gibbon, former researcher in the Ethnology Department of the Royal Ontario Museum, (ROM) and Elizabeth Blight, Head of the Still Images Division of the Provincial Archives of Manitoba, who discovered the connection between the Morris robes and their translations. I am grateful for their generosity in sharing this information. Thanks also to the staff of the ROM library who were cheerful and efficient in responding to my research requests, even when securing copies of books almost as rare as the buffalo robes themselves.

For their sustained support, I am grateful to Dr. Trudy Nicks and Dr. Jim McDonald, alternate curators-in-charge of the ROM's Ethnology Department. I am indebted as well to the two anonymous manuscript reviewers who, through the kind mediation of Dr. Peter Storck, Senior Editor of the ROM's Art and Archaeology Editorial Board, made valuable recommendations. Their input was a stimulus to further research and improved scholarship. Professor John C. Ewers, Curator Emeritus at the Smithsonian Institution, and Dr. Hugh A. Dempsey, Curator Emeritus at the Glenbow Museum, were extremely helpful in making corrections and suggestions and in providing additional information. For her significant contribution to the clarity and organization of the manuscript, and for her attention to detail, I wish to thank my editor, Andrea Gallagher Ellis.

The fine reproductions of the painted robes are the work of Brian Boyle of the ROM's Photography Department.

Finally, I am grateful to Virginia Morin, Designer, ROM Publications, for her sensitive and creative efforts; to Vickie Vasquez-O'Hara, Production Co-ordinator, who skilfully guided the book's production; and to Sandra Shaul, Head, and Glen Ellis, Managing Editor, who were early to recognize merit in this project and have given me their continued support.

BLACKFOOT PICTOGRAPHY AND THE MORRIS ROBES

AN ANALYSIS

INTRODUCTION

Between 1907 and 1911 the artist Edmund Morris travelled among the Plains Indians of Canada. His official purpose was to paint the portraits of the passing generation of Indian leaders, but perhaps more interesting today are the hundreds of photographs he took and the artifacts he collected. His travel diaries and correspondence contain a wealth of information about Plains Indian life, beliefs, and history. This study focuses on five painted buffalo robes—four Blackfoot and one Sarcee—donated by Morris to the Royal Ontario Museum in 1913. The robes bear the pictographic records of the brave deeds of eight veteran warriors: Running Wolf, Big Swan, Bull Plume, Leans Over Butchering,[1] Running Rabbit, Wolf Carrier, Bull Head, and Calf Child (see Figs. 1–8).

Morris commissioned these eight men to paint their war histories, in the "traditional manner" of picture-writing, on five buffalo hides, which he provided for the purpose. He also collected their translations of the depictions on the robes. The transcriptions were recorded in his diaries and correspondence. Since these buffalo hides were never worn in a traditional context, the term "robe" is somewhat of a misnomer; however, before being painted, the five hides were used in the Morris home in Toronto, probably as sleigh or carriage robes.[2] For the sake of precision it should be clear that the term "robe" as applied to the painted hides refers both to their use in the Morris home and to the intention of the collector, which was to obtain replicas of traditional war-exploit robes. As it turned out, no sooner had the paint dried than the five robes were returned to Toronto and hung in an exhibition, along with the Plains Indian portraits Morris had painted for the Ontario government and many of the artifacts he had collected, on the walls of the Canadian Art Club (see Morris 1909).

The lives of most of the painters spanned two phases of Blackfoot history, the nomadic days before the Treaty (No. 7, 1877) and the more sedentary life on the reserve. The primary goal of this study is to show how the robes reflect this period of transition in both artistic and social terms. In order to gain such insight the paintings are examined first as purely visual phenomena in relation to both traditional Blackfoot art and European art, and second, through a close look at the artists' lives and their immediate circumstances in order to appreciate why they may have chosen to follow one artistic tradition over another.

There are very specific difficulties encountered in the study of pictographic paintings on hide. The hides are generally large in size, measuring as much as 298 cm × 244 cm (9 feet, 10 inches × 8 feet). Since the traditional purpose of the hide or robe was to display the accumulation of the wearer's brave deeds, these large surfaces are usually densely covered with visual information. Consequently, figures on the robes tend to be small, and details that advance the narrative are even smaller. Sometimes the depictions lack definition because they were painted on particularly rough or absorbent hide. Over time, the paint has often undergone considerable deterioration. These difficulties, coupled with the fact that examples of pictographic robes are widely scattered in museums throughout Europe, Canada, and the United States, frustrate attempts to study the subtle and complex aspects of pictographic painting.

Photographs offer only a partial solution to this problem. Ideally, a single photograph should provide the means to contemplate the pictorial composition in its entirety as well as to focus on details. Because of the difficulties already noted, however, photographs are limited in their usefulness as tools for analysis.

In fact, it was through solving some of the technical difficulties that impede the analysis of pictographic paintings that I became interested in the paintings themselves. My first objective was simply to document the pictorial content of the Morris robes in order to supplement the ROM catalogue record. To reproduce the pictographic art on the robes, I developed and refined a

Figure 1 Running Wolf and Father Léon Doucet. Doucet, who had 39 years' experience living with the Blackfoot, was Morris' most important non-native contact in the area. Photograph by Edmund Morris, 1907. Courtesy Provincial Archives of Manitoba, Winnipeg, Edmund Morris Collection 18.

technique of tracing from the original onto clear plastic film with a felt pen, then photostatically reducing the image. At first, I used a black-and-white photocopier which could handle a maximum original paper size of 11 inches × 17 inches (280 mm × 432 mm); the process therefore involved dozens of intermediate "cut and paste" reductions in order to arrive at a final image that would fit onto letter-size paper. This proved to be remarkably accurate in preserving the scale of the originals and bringing all details into sharp focus, but the process was very labour-intensive. By turning over the task of reducing the tracings to professional photostat technicians, even more precise results were achieved with far less effort (see Pls. 1–5; Fig. 10). I found that the most economical and efficient method was to trace onto long sheets of film, 34 inches (87 cm) wide, then to scale down the image in two or three stages on a large-format photocopier, in this case a Xerox 5080.

Sometimes it was possible to execute the tracing by faithfully reproducing the thickness of the outlines on the original. At other times, it was necessary to produce thinner lines to avoid "plugging up" in the reduction process, so the outer edges of the outlines were used as a guide. One way or another, the figures and the relationships between figures are rendered true to scale. The primary difference between the reduced tracings and the original robes lies in colour reproduction. Since the reproductions were created for analytical purposes, the colours and outlines are sharper, more even, and brighter than on the original robes. Boldface Letraset™ numbers were added to connect the pictographic events on the robes with their written translations.

While the tracings provide an extremely useful study tool, the act of tracing the robes was itself a rewarding task. It was slow and careful work and required a close consideration of all the minute details of the robes, in some cases even allowing reconstruction of parts that were lost. During the course of tracing, the narrative and the visceral qualities of the painting sometimes became so vivid as to jolt me into a realization of how different and distant were the times captured by the artists. At other times, when a painter showed extraordinary draughtsmanship, I could only marvel at his skill as I replicated the movement of his "brush stroke" from the first contact of the paint-laden instrument with the hide to the completion of the stroke as the paint ran out.

In addition to deepening our understanding of Blackfoot culture, this study provides an opportunity to publish, for the first time, all five pictographic robes, both as photographs and as traced reproductions, along with their verbal translations.

Figure 2 Big Swan on the occasion of sitting for his portrait. Morris photographed many of his subjects at the same time as he rendered their portraits. Consequently, his photographs often show people in clothing usually reserved for ceremonial, traditional events. Photograph by Edmund Morris, 1907. Courtesy Provincial Archives of Manitoba, Winnipeg, Edmund Morris Collection 92.

Figure 3 Bull Plume (left) and Man Angry With Hunger. Photograph by Edmund Morris, 1907. Courtesy Provincial Archives of Manitoba, Winnipeg, Edmund Morris Collection 111.

Figure 4 Leans Over Butchering, from a photograph taken at the Lethbridge Fair in 1910. Courtesy Glenbow Archives, Calgary, NA 864-7.

Figure 5 In one of seventeen photographs Morris took of Running Rabbit's work in progress, Running Rabbit is shown gesturing with his "paint brush," a tool traditionally made from the porous section of a buffalo leg bone. Houghton, Running Rabbit's son and translator of the robe, sits with pen and paper in hand beside his father. Photograph by Edmund Morris, 1909. Courtesy Provincial Archives of Manitoba, Winnipeg, Edmund Morris Collection 195.

Figure 6 Blackfoot Sun Dance singers, 16 June 1913. Wolf Carrier is fifth from the left. Courtesy Glenbow Archives, Calgary, ND-24-45.

Figure 7 Bull Head (left) and Big Wolf. At the time, Bull Head was mourning the death of his nephew, Jim Big Plume, who was to have been his successor as head chief of the Sarcee (Morris 1985:28). Photograph by Edmund Morris, 1907. Courtesy Provincial Archives of Manitoba, Winnipeg, Edmund Morris Collection 540.

Figure 8 Calf Child sitting for his portrait with the ceremonial "Hailstone" painted tipi in the background (Brasser 1978:16). Photograph by Edmund Morris, 1907. Courtesy Provincial Archives of Manitoba, Winnipeg, Edmund Morris Collection 183.

THE TRADITIONAL ROLE OF PICTOGRAPHIC ROBES IN BLACKFOOT CULTURE

Our story begins not long before 1830 when the first recorded Blackfoot picto-graphic paintings came into European hands.[3] At that time the Algonkian-speaking Blackfoot Nation was composed of three tribes: the Pikuni or Peigan, the Kainai or Blood, and the Siksika or Blackfoot proper. Some one hundred years earlier, horses and guns first made their appearance in the Blackfoot ter-ritory of southern Alberta. Like the other Plains peoples, the Blackfoot fol-lowed a nomadic life based on the horse and buffalo. There was active sharing and trading within the Plains community as a whole, so Plains tribes had simi-lar religious beliefs, material culture, and warfare practices. Inter-tribal warfare and horse-raiding were dominant activities in the 19th century on the Plains (Grinnell 1892:244). Except for an alliance with the Algonkian-speaking Gros Ventre, which ended in 1861 (McGinnis 1974:16), and a more enduring alliance with the Athapaskan-speaking Sarcee, the Blackfoot were almost con-stantly at war with the neighbouring tribes: the Cree and the Assiniboine to the east, the Sioux and the Crow to the south, and the intermontane peoples, the Kootenay, the Flathead, the Shoshoni, and the Pend d'Oreille, to the west.

From a European perspective, inter-tribal conflict probably appeared more like competitive sport than warfare.[4] There is a certain validity to that perception since the objective of Plains Indian military tactics was not to inflict a large number of casualties; rather, it was to provide an arena in which great flourish could be expressed through battle manoeuvres and young men could achieve glory and recognition. The importance of inter-tribal warfare, however, reaches much deeper into the fabric of Plains Indian life.

Strength in supernatural power and skill on the warpath were inextricably connected and were essential to the successful warrior. War parties were usually initiated by an individual after he had sought supernatural power through either a vision or war medicine (Lewis 1942:56; Ewers 1958:127). As his accomplish-ments became known, the brave warrior and skilled horse-raider achieved politi-cal and economic prominence within his community (Wissler 1911:37; Kane 1858:126). His deeds were measured according to a system of "graded war hon-ours" (Smith 1938:429), sometimes called "coups," and were often recorded or registered. War exploits became the most prominent subject of Blackfoot pictographic art. Sometimes referred to as picture-writing, these records were painted on hide shirts, the outer walls of tipis, tipi liners, rock faces, and, most notably, skin robes.[5] The paintings enabled a successful warrior to advertise his achievements to the community at large (Ewers 1939:17). Warriors were often called upon to give detailed and animated verbal accounts (Grinnell 1892; Maclean 1896:109) of their brave deeds in social situations (Maclean 1896:110; Grinnell 1892:186) and on public occasions such as pipe ceremonies and processions (Wissler 1911:52; 1912:150, 153, 156), the Sun Dance (Grinnell 1892:267; Curtis 1911:45, 54; Point 1967:203), child-naming ceremonies (Wissler 1911:37), and ritual preparation for vision quests (Dempsey 1968:14). The literature does not seem to specify whether or not pictographic robes had a special function in such recitations. One may speculate, however, that, since veracity was extremely important in recounting exploits (Grinnell 1892:219, 249; 1910:300; Dempsey 1980:118; Catlin 1851, 1:148 *in* Dunn 1968:137), the painted robes acted as a mnemonic device. We may also draw inference from Father Nicolas Point's experience during the 1840s, when he showed religious paintings to the Blackfoot, in order to "impress the Indians very vividly" with the stories of the gospel (Point 1967:94). We may imagine a warrior reciting his brave deeds in the same way, pointing to the pictures on his robe to make a greater impression on his listeners (Hall 1926:8). Beyond self-aggrandizement we can only speculate on the function of pictographic robes; however, it is evident that Blackfoot pictorial painting was influenced by, and attuned to, a number of factors acting within a larger cultural framework.

Two almost simultaneous events, the signing of Treaty No. 7 in 1877 and the disappearance of the buffalo, marked an abrupt change in Blackfoot culture. Although the practice of painting war-exploit robes in the traditional sense appears to have been discontinued after settlement on reserves, the verbal recitation of brave war deeds persisted as a significant part of ceremonies and social occasions. It would seem that wherever possible traditional ways were continued as an important source of spiritual nourishment and social cohesion for the Blackfoot. However, subsistence and, to a large degree, political leadership of the tribe came to be based on cooperation with the church and the government, both of which had their sights set on assimilating the Indians, which meant for the most part eradicating their traditions. These circumstances were very much at play during the period 1907–11, when Edmund Morris visited the reserves of the Blackfoot.

COLLECTION HISTORY OF
THE MORRIS ROBES

Edmund Morris' deep interest in native culture undoubtedly finds its roots in Fort Garry, Manitoba, where his father, Alexander Morris, served as Lieutenant Governor of the districts of Manitoba, Assiniboia, Keewatin, and the North West Territories in the 1870s. As the principal government negotiator of Indian treaties in the prairies, Morris senior frequently hosted visiting Indian leaders, who must have left a lasting impression on his young son. Later, Edmund Morris (Fig. 9) became greatly concerned that the traditions of Plains Indians were rapidly disappearing,[6] and set about compiling a record of their ways. He began in 1907, at the age of thirty-six, to execute a series of pastel portraits of Plains Indians commissioned by the government of Ontario. Soon after, he received commissions from the Saskatchewan and Alberta governments. During the period 1907–11, he gathered some four hundred artifacts,[7] completed almost 135 portraits,[8] took more than six hundred photographs on Plains reserves, maintained a diary, and kept up a lively correspondence with Indian agents, missionaries, Indian leaders, and friends. In 1913, the year of his death, Morris donated his collection of artifacts, one of his diaries, and his ethnographic library to the Royal Ontario Museum. In the same year, the government of Ontario transferred its collection of sixty Morris portraits to the ROM. The photographs, another diary, and the bulk of his correspondence regarding Canadian Indians are preserved in the Provincial Archives of Manitoba, Winnipeg.[9]

Through contacts established by his father, Edmund Morris was able to gain assistance from an impressive array of individuals having vast knowledge of Plains Indian culture and western Canadian history. In addition, Morris was aided by a number of Indian agents supervised by his friend Duncan Campbell Scott, who at the time was the Assistant Superintendent of Indian Affairs. Because of these excellent connections, a great number of the items in the ROM's Edmund Morris Collection are associated with Indian leaders who were active in pre-Treaty days, and many of the objects were presented by Indian leaders as gifts to Morris. In addition to reflecting the generosity of the leaders and perhaps their esteem for Morris and his father, these presentations may signify the Indians' intent to bolster their positions as leaders or their hope that Morris would use his political influence on their behalf to increase the food rations from Ottawa and to alleviate the pressure to sell reserve lands.

While the Morris material stands as a truly significant scholarly contribution to ethnology, it also reflects certain biases on the part of the collector. First, Morris was primarily interested in a phase of Blackfoot history that ended about fifty years before his visits; as a result, the information he recorded, often through a translator, relied solely on the memories of others. For example, Morris asked John Three Bulls to paint a robe bearing the war history of his famous uncle, the then-deceased Head Chief Crowfoot. In making such a request, however, Morris was apparently running contrary to Blackfoot tradition: in the words of Chief Yellow Horse, "A man can only record his own history according to custom" (Morris 1985:158).[10] Second, Morris' view was somewhat tinted by a romantic notion of past native culture. In his own words, "It is what the Indians were, & what a noble life they had, roaming the plains after the game & living in their lodges of buffalo skins rich in the robes of this animal, and how superbly they fit into the surrounding landscape that interests so many of us" (Morris 1985:122). Third, he was not beyond taking artistic licence at the expense of ethnographic accuracy. He admitted guilt in this regard when he wrote to his sculptor friend, Phimister Proctor, "Now about the Indian suits I got them to use in my pictures the American ["Natural" crossed out] Archeological Museum ["or Mr. Grinnell"[11] crossed out] will hang me."[12] Finally, Morris was influenced by prevailing notions in anthropology. In particular, the importance that anthropologists placed on preserving a record of "pure" physical types, in the form of photographs and

Figure 9 Edmund Morris (right) and Peter Erasmus, who translated the events portrayed on Calf Child's robe. Erasmus was an important figure in Canadian history. He was a guide on the Palliser Expedition, 1857–60, a translator for the Indians during negotiations for Treaty No. 6 at Fort Carlton and Fort Pitt in 1876, and largely instrumental in creating the first Cree dictionary and syllabary (Morris 1985:107). Photograph by Edmund Morris, 1909. Courtesy Provincial Archives of Manitoba, Winnipeg, Edmund Morris Collection 253.

plaster casts, seems to have influenced the way he selected and posed his models. Concerning the painting of the five robes, Morris again followed an anthropological practice by commissioning Indian craftsmen to make replicas of objects that had fallen out of use in their culture.

Among Morris' papers in the Provincial Archives of Manitoba there is a photograph of a painted robe depicting the life of Many Shots, a Blackfoot. The robe, along with its translation, was collected by Reverend John Maclean, a Methodist missionary. In 1894 Maclean published the robe, numerically keying the pictured exploits to their verbal explanations (Maclean 1894).[13] Morris adopted this basic structure when he recorded translations of the pictographic representations and placed numbers on the robes. An example of a deer hide painted in the early Blackfoot style (Fig. 10) was the subject of one of several articles devoted to picture-

Figure 10 Photograph (above) and tracing (right) of a painted deerskin in the early Blackfoot style, probably collected in the late 1800s. Traditionally, a quillwork strip decorated the "spine" of painted war-exploit robes. Down the centre of this skin is painted instead a snake-like creature that bears a horn on its head (Ewers 1981:44; Ted J. Brasser, personal communication, 1989). Royal Ontario Museum, Toronto, 975x73.6.

writing that appeared in the *Annual Archaeological Report* of 1904 and 1905 (Boyle 1904). The painted deer hide, now in the ROM, was collected by Sarah Curzon, head of the Toronto Women's Historical Society. The article was written by David Boyle, Provincial Archaeologist of Ontario, and included a letter from the collector's daughter, Edith Curzon, in which she described her unsuccessful attempt to have a photograph of this pictographic deerskin interpreted while visiting the North Blackfoot reserve. It is almost certain that Morris knew the Curzons and that he had read Boyle's article on the Blackfoot deer hide; these circumstances, together with Maclean's article, likely contributed to Morris' interest in securing examples of war-exploit robes, along with their translations, from the Blackfoot.

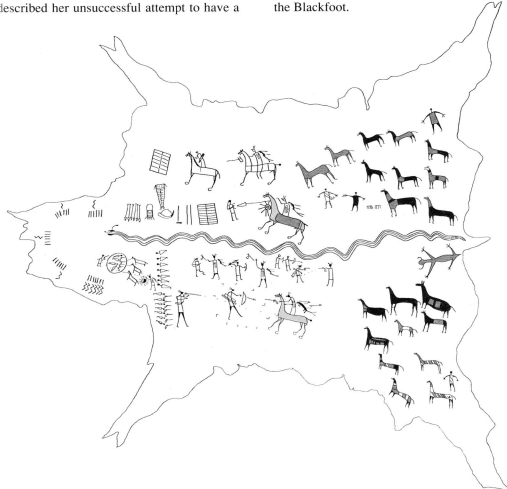

TRADITIONAL BLACKFOOT PICTOGRAPHY AND THE MORRIS ROBES

The Blackfoot system of graded war honours, war medicine, and regalia differed somewhat from those of other Plains peoples. In the same way, their pictographic art maintained certain distinct tribal traditions, which may be considered as variations within the general theme of Plains Indian pictography.

With regard to the Blackfoot, Reverend John Maclean, who laboured among the Blood from 1878 to 1888, was informed that "when the South Peigan visited these rocks [a set of petroglyphs in Montana] they used them as models when they returned home, drawing figures on robes similar to those they had seen" (Maclean 1896:118).[14] Indeed, the forms of "V-neck warriors" and "shield-bearing warriors," which are so prominent in rock art of the northwest Plains (see Conner and Conner 1971:20), do appear in the earliest documented Blackfoot hide paintings, dated to the 1830s.[15] The distribution of the V-neck figure is largely restricted to Montana and the very southern part of Alberta.[16] These figures are also found, probably in greater numbers, in Crow hide paintings from around 1850.[17] The Crow V-necks have an elongated, ballet-like quality (Fig. 11), which distinguishes them from the stockier, less mobile, Blackfoot figures (Fig. 12). Shield-bearing warriors,[18] figures whose torsos are replaced by large circular shields, appear less frequently in Blackfoot hide paintings than the V-neck figures. However, since a panel of shield-bearing warriors was recently dated to A.D. 1104 (Loendorf 1990:45), the appearance of these figures in Blackfoot pictography is significant: it suggests continuity with a northwestern Plains artistic tradition of great antiquity.[19]

As mentioned earlier, a note in Garry (1900:203) referring to the acquisition of two Blackfoot robes seems to be the earliest record of such items coming into European hands. The robes were probably collected in the 1820s and, although they appear to be no longer extant, Garry's description of them confirms the autobiographical nature of Blackfoot war-exploit robes:

1 Buffalo Robe. Present from "Painted Feather", a Slave [Blackfoot] Indian Chief, adorned with Human Hair from Scalps of 11 of his Enemies whom

he had killed in Battle; painted by himself and a Piece of Red Cloth taken from a Stone [Assiniboine] Indian with his Hair—killed in Battle.

1 Ornamental Buffalo Robe. A Present from a Slave [Blackfoot] Indian Chief, "Bull's Back Fat", with a Painting inside depicting his dangerous Situation when surrounded by his Enemies from whom he miraculously escaped. [Garry 1900:203][20]

In order to discern in greater detail features that characterize traditional Blackfoot pictography, we turn to a collection of nine robes and four shirts, designated the Early Set (see Appendix), for which we do have visual records. These are perhaps the only surviving examples of Blackfoot hide paintings of war exploits made exclusively for native use before settlement on reserves. Several of the robes exist only in the form of facsimiles drawn by European artists, and one exists only as a photograph. Overall, the accompanying documentation tends to be incomplete. In spite of these limitations, this set of works is useful in providing a basis for defining Blackfoot pictographic painting as a distinct, tribal tradition. Furthermore, the Early Set serves as a reference for measuring the influence of European art on that of the Blackfoot.

Each painting in the Early Set displays the war exploits accomplished by the robe's or shirt's owner over the course of his career as a warrior. In other words, each war shirt or hide robe provides a frame around numerous events that occurred at different times and places.

Among the examples two distinct types of war-honour depictions may be discerned: Type 1 is a register or display of inanimate objects, apparently representing brave deeds. Type 2 shows human figures in the act of achieving war honours. The four Type 1 examples (Appendix, Early Set, j–m) show almost no concern for physical action and are mainly a tabulatory record, with rows of weapons, such as guns, lances, bows and arrows, clubs, and shields, along with other objects, including scalps, blankets, and pouches.[21] Additional rows of minimally delineated, inactive human forms are found on two examples of these four (j–k). The remaining nine examples of the Early Set (a–i) belong in Type 2 and display warriors in action, such as taking weapons and killing enemies. Six of the Type 2 paintings (Early Set, e–i) contain, more or less, discrete sub-sections devoted to a tally of objects

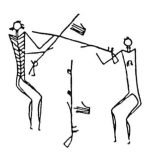

Figure 11 V-neck figures from a Crow painted buffalo robe dating to 1838. Bernisches Historisches Museum, Bern, N.A.4.

Figure 12 V-neck figures from an undocumented Blackfoot painted buffalo robe probably from the early 19th century. Musée de l'Homme, Paris, 96.73.1.

17

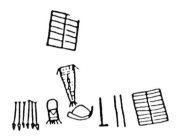

Figure 13 Tally of objects from an early Blackfoot painted deerskin (detail, Fig. 10).

Figure 14 Tally of objects and figures from Running Rabbit's robe (Pl. 2, scene 8).

Figure 15 Various ways of depicting scalps on the Morris robes.

equivalent to those represented in Type 1 (Fig. 13). One robe (e) shows an equal division of the two types of depictions.

Systems of graded war honours differed from one tribe to the next. Although the precise details of the Blackfoot system have not been firmly established,[22] it is evident that, in comparison with other tribes, the Blackfoot placed greater emphasis on the capture of weapons and other objects. Perhaps this distinct feature of the Blackfoot system of graded war honours explains the appearance of object tabulations found in their pictographs.[23] Since such tabulations tend not to appear in the paintings of other Plains cultures, it is possible that they are a characteristic feature of Blackfoot pictographic art.

While there appear to be no surviving examples of Type 1 war histories painted after the first half of the 19th century, the Blackfoot continued to produce Type 2 paintings until very recent times. In order to supplement this study of the Morris robes, I reviewed thirteen war-exploit paintings (three tipis and ten robes) executed in the period between settlement on reserves (1877) and the time of the Morris commission (1909). These have been designated the Later Set (see Appendix). Nine of the thirteen include discrete tabulations of objects. Three of the Morris robes, those of Wolf Carrier, Bull Head, and Running Rabbit (Pls. 2–4), bear such tallies (Fig. 14).

Looking at the entire corpus of Blackfoot paintings, in both narrative and tabulatory contexts, inanimate objects tend to be drawn in a naturalistic and graphic manner. In some cases there is a tendency towards geometrical abstraction. For example, scalps were variously depicted as fringed rectangles, such as those found on Running Rabbit's robe (Pl. 2) and in several early robes (Appendix, Early Set, h–i); as comb shapes, as on Calf Child's robe (Pl. 5) and two early robes (Early Set, e, i); and as fringed circles, such as those on the robes of Wolf Carrier (Pl. 3) and the Four Peigan Chiefs (Pl. 1), as well as in several of the early examples (Early Set, d, j). It is possible that some of these variations (Fig. 15), particularly the fringed rectangle, are unique Blackfoot conventions. Another abstracted form, the circular entrenched battle, is found in several variations in early paintings as well as on the Morris robes. It may be that several of these entrenched battle forms were also unique Blackfoot pictorial conventions.[24]

Aside from their function in tallies, inanimate objects were widely used among most Plains tribes, including the Blackfoot, to advance the narrative in pictographic paintings. The early paintings usually depicted man-to-man combat with the weapons of each fighter clearly delineated. No doubt these weapons had a mnemonic function, identifying specific events and individuals.

In the early pictographs (Early Set, a, c–d, h) weapons often appear to be floating next to warrior figures, touching or almost touching the head or upper torso (Fig. 16). The significance of such weapons within the narrative of these encounters is often ambiguous. For example, the meaning of a bow poised above a warrior's head is open to several possible interpretations: a bow has been captured, an enemy has been killed with a bow, or the victor has counted coup with a bow by touching the enemy under dangerous conditions. Furthermore, in these cases it is not always clear who is the defeated and who is the victor. In attempting to interpret such scenes we might bear in mind that in contrast to neighbouring tribes the Blackfoot war-honour system appears to have given less accreditation to the counting of coup than to the capture of weapons.

Weapons were not the only inanimate objects used as narrative devices. A particular piece of regalia sometimes served to identify the hero or the enemy. Calf Child is identified by an elaborate horned and feathered headdress and shield in several events on his robe (Fig. 17), as is the hero in the robe copied by Karl Bodmer in 1833 (Thomas and Ronnefeldt 1976:17) and in several other Blackfoot robes (Appendix, Early Set, e, h; Later Set, b, e). In connection with the Blackfoot and the Crow, Catlin noted and sketched "curious appendages to the persons or wardrobes of an Indian . . . sometimes made of the skin of an otter, a beaver, . . . sometimes the skin of an animal so large as a wolf" (Catlin 1876:37, pls. 14, 18–19). Decorated skins, likely a form of war medicine, are shown hanging from behind the head or neck of the hero in three of the early Blackfoot robes (Early Set, e, h–i; see also Fig. 18) and in at least three of the later paintings (Later Set, b, e, i). I have been able to locate only two or three non-Blackfoot war paintings that bear such war-medicine skins.[25]

Objects functioning as ideograms were effective in carrying the narrative in Blackfoot pictography. Metonymy, the substitution of one thing to signify another (Hoffman 1895:45), for example, rifles standing for warriors holding rifles, and synecdoche, the "substitution of part of an object or idea for the whole" (Hoffman 1895:47) were probably the most common ideographic conventions employed by the Blackfoot. The detached-hand ideogram may be found in most of the early paintings as well as on the Morris robes; it usually

Figure 16 Warrior figures with "floating" weapons, from an undocumented robe in the early Blackfoot style (detail, Fig. 12).

Figure 17 Calf Child is depicted in his battle regalia, from Calf Child's robe (Pl. 5, scene 3).

Figure 18 Warrior with war-medicine skin, from a painted deerskin in the early Blackfoot style (detail, Fig. 10).

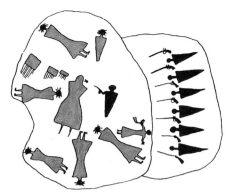

Figure 19 The image to the right of the central woman's head signifies the scalp taken by the triangular warrior figure holding a gun. Three scalps are represented to her left. To her right, the detached forearm grasping the girl's wrist signifies that Running Rabbit took her captive. From Running Rabbit's robe (Pl. 2, scene 1).

Figure 20 These abstract images are not true symbols, but rather graphic illustrations. They signify the number of times that Wolf Carrier had been a scout and sighted the enemy. The arc portion represents the war party as they await the scout's return. "The warriors stood in a semi-circle and sang while the scout approached" (Dempsey 1980:42). The zig-zag stands for the path taken by the scout to conceal the position of his compatriots (McClintock 1936:24; Marquis 1928:125; Curtis 1909:108; Ewers 1944:187). From Wolf Carrier's robe (Pl. 3, scenes 3–4).

implies the act of capturing an object or, less frequently, a person (Fig. 19). The appearance of this hand is often the only clue that distinguishes the victor from the vanquished. An example on Running Rabbit's robe (Pl. 2, scene 10) shows a detached-hand image used to signify the theft of a horse tethered to a tipi, an act worthy of specific accreditation in the Blackfoot system of graded war honours. That this particular war honour does not seem to appear in the Early Set of paintings, yet is found on all but one in the Later Set (b), may indicate that the act of stealing a tethered horse came into greater prominence in the later years of inter-tribal warfare. The abstract symbol standing for an accredited scouting mission (Fig. 20) seems to be a distinctive Blackfoot convention. Again, this particular form is found exclusively on later paintings. It is possible, however, that these are variations of somewhat similar forms found on several of the early examples (Appendix, Early Set, b, d, h–j). In general, ideographic devices were used extensively by the Blackfoot and they were usually in the form of depictions of real objects rather than true abstract symbols (Fig. 21; Mallery 1889:286).

From the earliest-known Blackfoot pictographs to the most recent, complex scenes embrace several connected events in which the hero executes brave deeds at several places and points in time.[26] For example, Running Rabbit combined spatially and temporally distinct sequences into a single graphic unity on scene 10 of his robe (Fig. 22; see Petersen 1971:11, 272). Dotted lines standing for paths of flying bullets, lines of dashes representing footprints, and repeated U-shapes tracing the trail of a horse are the connecting devices that allow one to read the sequence of events occurring within complex scenes. These ideographic devices occur in the pictographic paintings of most Plains tribes.

Plains draughtsmen viewed the surface of the buffalo robe in terms of multiple vantage points, and their treatment of pictorial space was fundamentally two-dimensional. This fidelity to the inherent flatness of the picture plane is reflected in the absence of pictorial conventions that would suggest the third dimension.

Overlap, which probably "provides the best cue, with the least ambiguity, to the percept of depth" (Deregowski 1984:115), is all but absent in the early paintings. Figures and objects were rendered in outline, side by side, and one on top of the other, and rarely did these forms overlap. An interesting problem with respect to overlap may be found in the depiction of mounted warriors.

Riders were apparently never shown astride their horses, that is, with one leg visible in front and the other partly hidden behind the mount. In the early paintings, and on some of the Morris robes, mounted riders were variously represented with torso and no legs (Appendix, Early Set, e, i; Running Rabbit's robe, Pl. 2 scene 4); with the torso visible above the horse and two legs visible beneath (Early Set, b, e); or with complete bodies of both rider and horse displayed at once (Early Set, a, h; Bull Head's robe, Pl. 4, scene 5; Wolf Carrier's robe, Pl. 3, scene 9). The last example illustrates a convention known as "transparency," in which all features are brought to the surface of the picture plane (Figs. 23–25).

Blackfoot pictographs were essentially tabulatory devices showing little concern for three-dimensional pictorial space. In the same vein, perhaps the Blackfoot viewed their pictographs fundamentally differently than the way in which a person conditioned to European conventions of pictorial space looks at an oil painting. In fact, there are reasons to believe that the Blackfoot regarded their pictorial works in a way more akin to viewing a map. As in a map, the sizes of figures are scaled to conform to a flat surface rather than to illusionary three-dimensional space. The Blackfoot tendency to distribute figures, or groups of figures, evenly over the painting surface gave greater visual access to the deeds tabulated on the robe and further confirmed the two-dimensional nature of the picture plane. On the other hand, a viewer conditioned to interpret pictorial space according to the conventions of European-style perspective will tend to interpret figures higher in the picture

Figure 21 Wolf Carrier graphically indicated that he was wounded in the foot and the cheek. From Wolf Carrier's robe (Pl. 3, scene 13).

Figure 22 A scene narrated in six sequences. From right to left: 1. Running Rabbit is riding with a war party towards a Crow camp. 2. Running Rabbit, identified by the "take" sign over his shoulder, is off his horse. 3. Footprints follow his path to a Crow tipi. 4. The detached hand holding a knife indicates the cutting of one tether and the line through the other shows that it too has been cut. 5. A single footprint and a "take" sign identify Running Rabbit as the individual on the stolen horse. 6. Running Rabbit is standing in front of a herd representing the accumulation of horses he stole from the Crow in his lifetime. From Running Rabbit's robe (Pl. 2, scene 10).

Figure 23 In the early paintings the rider was sometimes shown in full, overlapping the horse except for the outlines. From Wolf Carrier's robe (Pl. 3, scene 6).

Figure 24 The convention of transparency enabled Wolf Carrier to economically illustrate his stealing a rifle inside the tipi of an enemy, one of the most highly accredited of the Blackfoot graded war honours. From Wolf Carrier's robe (Pl. 3, scene 15).

Figure 25 The two lead horses in Running Rabbit's encounter with the Cree are shown with all features brought to the surface of the picture plane. From Running Rabbit's robe (Pl. 2, scene 9).

plane as being farther away: "Elevation in the field of view is one of the most universally established and strongest of depth cues" (Deregowski 1980:36). In European perspective a sense of depth is further enhanced by diminishing the size of objects as they move up the picture plane. In contrast, the Blackfoot tended to make the figures on a robe of uniform size. Scenes in later paintings seem to embrace an increased number of figures, but size uniformity and the even dispersal of figures continued to reinforce the essential two-dimensional quality of Blackfoot pictographs (Figs. 26–27).

In early Blackfoot paintings, and to a large extent in the Morris robes, figures and scenes were presented in their most typical views. For example, humans were usually depicted with the head and torso shown frontally and the legs and feet rotated unnaturally ninety degrees, not unlike the schematized "walk" figure on our street lights. Some scenes encompassing a large number of figures were rendered from a bird's-eye view, while figures included therein were depicted from eye level (Figs. 28–29). This "blending of typical views" (Eng 1931:129) throws off any attempt to control space in the manner of linear perspective (Deregowski 1984:64) and further serves to flatten pictorial space.

In both the early paintings and the Morris robes, Blackfoot artists tended to schematize the human form into abstract, geometrical shapes. Figures with triangular torsos and no legs (Fig. 30), and triangular figures terminating in a single leg and foot (Fig. 31) are the most common schematized human forms on the Morris robes. The latter variation is found in considerable numbers in the early paintings (Appendix, Early Set, b, f, h–j) and is often in context with representations of entrenched battle scenes. In Blackfoot art triangular figures were usually shown without arms or with only one arm. These particular variations of triangular-torsoed figures seem to be absent from the pictographs of other Plains tribes. However, figures with rectangular torsos, varying from four-limbed to limbless, predominate in the older paintings. Rectangular-torsoed figures also appear in early paintings from other Plains cultures, but there seem to be distinguishing features. The Blackfoot variations tend to be notably more stocky and less robust and are surmounted by a single line to represent the neck. The Blackfoot "V-neck" figures appear to be a variation of the rectangular-torsoed form. The internal areas of the torso were sometimes painted with geometrical patterns, particularly open cross-hatching, stripes, and repeated chevrons, a practice also found in the paint-

Figure 26 The names Blood, Many Horses, and Bull Head were probably inscribed on this scene at Morris' request. From Bull Head's robe (Pl. 4, scene 1).

Figure 28 In some cultures, planes supporting upright figures were freely tilted without altering the implicit understanding that the figures remained vertical (Fortes 1948; Reuning and Wortley 1973:73). From Calf Child's robe (Pl. 5, scene 9).

Figure 27 The pair of black figures is shown surrounded by a war party of Crow warriors. The figures' splayed feet, empty hands at their sides, and bilateral symmetry form a unity of visual and gestural language that conveys a sense of helplessness and immobility. From Running Rabbit's robe (Pl. 2, scene 4).

Figure 29 From Calf Child's robe (Pl. 5, scene 10).

Figure 30 In this battle scene Bull Plume depicted both triangular and rectangular warrior figures. From the robe of the Four Peigan Chiefs (Pl. 1, scene 3a).

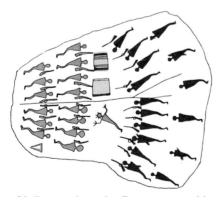

Figure 31 Repeated warrior figures arranged in a symmetrical pattern. The conventionalized figures may relate to the stance of the military dancers of the Dove Society (Dunn 1968:16; Farr 1984:88) or to the One Legged Dance of the Plains Ojibwa (Wolfe 1988:62). Then again, they may also represent mounted warriors, since the body position bears a resemblance to that of a rider on a horse. From Running Rabbit's robe (Pl. 2, scene 5).

ings of the Hidatsa and Crow. That the rectangular-torsoed form persisted in Blackfoot pictographs is readily apparent on four of the Morris robes (those of the Four Peigan Chiefs, Running Rabbit, Wolf Carrier, and Calf Child, Pls. 1–3, 5). Torsos were always surmounted by a head, depicted as a featureless, regularly shaped circle, sometimes with a conventionalized coiffure or headdress. Hands, when depicted, tended to be shown with outstretched fingers represented by radiating lines. In comparison with early Crow, Mandan, and Sioux robes, the figures on early Blackfoot pictographs and on the Morris robes appear much less animated in their movements (Figs. 32–33). Blackfoot figures were often symmetrical, with torsos displayed frontally and almost always with straight legs. These characteristics combine to give an appearance of immobility.

Anything added to the human form in the way of clothing and accessories was kept to a minimum; when present, such objects seem to convey specific information rather than to serve as decoration. The colour palette in the early works usually consisted of red, yellow, black, and green (Wied *in* Vatter 1927:51). By and large, the Morris robes reflect the same colour range. A wedge-shaped implement, carved from the spongy part of a buffalo's leg bone, was used to apply the paint on the early robes and on at least one of the Morris robes, that of Running Rabbit (Fig. 5).

Horses appear on almost all of the early war-exploit paintings. Like humans, horses were drawn in a highly conventionalized manner, but the tendency was not so much in the direction of geometrical representation as towards an exaggeration of the most distinctive features of the animal (Petersen 1971:18). Horses were shown as long and slender through the girth, neck, and head (Keyser 1977:33), probably to emphasize speed as a desirable characteristic (Fig. 34). Unlike human figures, horses were always rendered in full profile. In the early paintings hoofs were almost always represented by C- or U-shaped hooks, which, in turn, resemble horse tracks. Like humans, the bodies of horses sometimes bore internal geometrical markings and almost always held stationary poses. Aside from horses, the only animals to appear on the early paintings are two buffalos (Appendix, Early Set, h) and several supernatural creatures (Early Set, d, i). Two buffalos and one bear were the only animals other than horses represented on the Morris robes from the Blackfoot.

In general, the manner of depicting form in the early Blackfoot paintings and the Morris robes seems in harmony with the robe as a tabulatory and mnemonic device. In this context the use of conventionalized, often symmetrical, human forms constantly repeated and configured into patterns is appropriate since "symmetry creates stability and cohesion which, in turn, enhances memorability" (Deregowski 1984:66; Fig. 32).

The function of the robe as a record of events is further enhanced by the frequent use of ideographic devices, the two-dimensional approach to pictorial space, and the diachronic treatment of time. These characteristics of Blackfoot pictorials, coupled with their expression of culturally enshrined aesthetic conventions, are significantly different from the formal characteristics associated with contemporaneous European painting.

There are several other features of hide paintings that are only marginally related to this discussion of traditional elements in Blackfoot pictography. An intricate quillwork or beadwork band stitched down the centre of the hide is found on six of the nine robes from the Early Set (a, d, g–h, l–m; see Appendix). Neither the Morris robes nor the robes included in the Later Set bear this embellishment. Unlike the Morris robes, the early pictographic skin robes retain a vestige of the leg and head and sometimes the tail areas of the animal.[27]

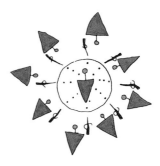

Figure 32 The Blackfoot consistently drew highly stylized configurations to represent entrenched battles. Their symmetrical form gives rise to a static appearance. From Wolf Carrier's robe (Pl. 3, scene 2).

Figure 33 The frontal treatment of straight-legged figures imparts a sense of motionlessness in Bull Plume's confrontation with a group of Kootenay Indians. From the robe of the Four Peigan Chiefs (Pl. 1, scene 4).

Figure 34 The "fine white horse" captured by Bull Plume is characteristic of the earlier style of painting, whereas the corral incorporates some elements of perspective drawing. From the robe of the Four Peigan Chiefs (Pl. 1, scene 3b).

EUROPEAN INFLUENCES ON THE MORRIS ROBES

In contrast to traditional Blackfoot pictographic painters, 19th-century European artists conceived of painting as a process inextricably tied to the act of seeing. Consequently, European artists embraced certain pictorial conventions: illusion of three-dimensional space through linear perspective and foreshortening; the modelling of forms through the use of shading; studied fidelity to anatomical and architectural features; and use of a wide range of colours and finely divided hues. Along with these visual characteristics, European pictures tended to embrace a synchronic notion of time: they preserve the integrity of time and space in the same way that a photograph does.

There were a number of opportunities for traditional Blackfoot war painters to adopt European pictorial conventions. In the Hudson's Bay Company records there is a recommendation, presumably dating to around 1820, that traders distribute among Plains Indians, likely including the Blackfoot, small paintings on metal depicting animal scenes.[28] The first trained European artist to work among the Blackfoot was Karl Bodmer, a meticulous draughtsman who accompanied Prince Maximilian of Wied on his scientific expedition to the upper Missouri in 1833 (see Thomas and Ronnefeldt 1976). Other artists to work among the Blackfoot before 1850 include George Catlin (see Catlin 1851, 1876, 1926), Paul Kane (see Kane 1858), and Alfred Miller. The Blackfoot observed these artists at work with a great deal of interest. Father Nicolas Point, who initiated the first missionary activity among the Blackfoot in 1846, was an amateur artist and was admitted into at least one Blackfoot village solely because the chiefs derived so much pleasure in having their portraits painted in full regalia (Point 1967:14). Despite this exposure, however, there is little, if any, evidence that European pictorial conventions influenced Blackfoot war paintings before 1850.[29]

European trade goods on the other hand were the cause of some changes in the first half of the 19th century. New colours were added to the Blackfoot palette (see Miller, Moffatt, and Sirois 1990:7–13), and blankets, guns, and powder horns appeared with greater frequency on Blackfoot paintings. In

1859 a trader from Fort Edmonton remarked that the Blackfoot "are rapidly adopting blankets and capots, and are giving up the beautifully painted robes of their forefathers. The few robes that are now made are inferior in workmanship to those of days gone by" (Ewers 1968:8). It is not clear, however, whether this decline applies to war-exploit robes or to other forms of painted robes. In the 1860s and 1870s European settlement pushed the eastern Plains tribes towards the Rockies, forcing them into a smaller land base. For example, the Sioux were forced into closer proximity with the Blackfoot and, as a result, fighting between the two intensified. Shifts in human populations, coupled with the need to exist on a diminishing supply of buffalo, may have wrought changes in Blackfoot warfare and, by extension, in war-exploit painting, but such speculations have yet to be confirmed.

When inter-tribal warfare ended and the buffalo herds disappeared in the last quarter of the 19th century, the effect of European contact on Blackfoot war paintings became more pronounced. At least three of the later paintings were executed on steer hides (Appendix, Later Set, c, g, i), while, like those commissioned by Morris, two if not more were painted on "recycled" buffalo hides (d, f), and on three hides (e–f, j) the pictographic images are interspersed with geometrical painting. Pictographic painting was traditionally strictly a male activity, whereas geometrical designs (Fig. 35) were painted exclusively by women. Very seldom are the two types of painting found in combination. Only one Blackfoot robe (Later Set, e) appears to combine geometrical and pictorial images simultaneously. Three other robes (Early Set, d; Later Set, f, i) appear to have been originally painted with geometric designs and overlaid at a later date with pictographic war-exploit paintings.[30] One of the pictographic hides in the Later Set (d) was painted on what had formerly been a tipi liner, and at least four of the Later Set (c–d, g, k) were collected with translations of the picture-writing, some of which are as detailed as those accompanying the Morris robes. Morris, however, went a step further by asking that lines be drawn around individual events and that numbers be inscribed to correlate each event with its translation. The figures on early painted hides tended to be uni-directional so that all the events were right side up when the robe was worn. In contrast, on three of the Morris robes and on eight of those in the Later Set the alignment of figures seems to vary as the painter worked his way around the perimeter of the hide. Initials or names inscribed next to the hero appear on two of the Morris robes (Bull

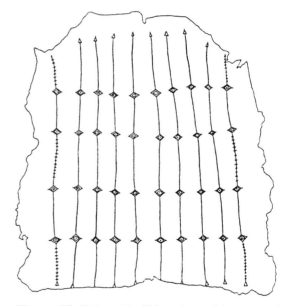

Figure 35 Painted buffalo robes with geometric designs featuring parallel lines and arrow-like forms seem to have been popular among the Blackfoot and Cree in the first half of the 19th century. This illustration was made by tracing from the original, which was documented by the collector, Edmund Morris, as an "ancient Cree robe." Royal Ontario Museum, Toronto, HK458.

Figure 36 Running Wolf was in many ways a traditionalist, but his drawing style was very much influenced by European pictures. His drawing shows how the layering of planes, particularly in the overlapping of the legs, gives a strong sense of the third dimension. He identified himself in his exploits by placing his initials above his head. From the robe of the Four Peigan Chiefs (Pl. 1, scene 1c).

Figure 37 The tipis drawn by Leans Over Butchering show European influence in the use of overlap. Painted tipis were traditionally reserved for only a few important individuals, yet almost all Chief Butcher's tipis, including those from this detail, show decoration. From the robe of the Four Peigan Chiefs (Pl. 1, scene 5).

Head's and the Four Peigan Chiefs') as well as on one robe from the Later Set (h). Five of the ten robes in the Later Set (b–d, f–g) appear to have been made for sale.

Two of the three painted war-exploit tipis in the Later Set (j–k) are known to recount the deeds of a number of individuals. While this may be a traditional practice with regard to Blackfoot tipi painting, the early war-exploit robes and shirts are thought to display the deeds of the wearer only. In contrast, the robe of the Four Peigan Chiefs commissioned by Morris displays the war histories of several individuals.

Another break with tradition is the increased number of horses found on the later robes. This change may reflect a shift away from prestige acquired through acts of bravery and towards prestige derived from wealth in horses (Lewis 1942:58; Mishkin 1940:61–62). Also, assorted animals other than horses receive greater prominence on the robes in the Later Set (b–e, g).

Content aside, there are certain formal aspects of the Morris robes that show European influence. While the Morris robes remain fundamentally planar, there are a number of images shown in three dimensions. Although two images suggest perspective (Pl. 4, scene 10; possibly Fig. 34), the illusion of depth on the Morris robes was largely achieved through the overlapping of forms (Figs. 36–37). Many of the equestrian warriors are shown astride their horses, with the leg of the rider overlapping the horse. On the other hand, non-overlapping figures, of approximately equal size and evenly distributed over the picture plane, give the Morris robes a two-dimensional quality much like that of the earlier robes. Unlike the earlier examples, however, in several cases the size of figures varies considerably, either on an arbitrary basis or in accordance with the needs of the narrative, for example, an important individual may be drawn larger than the rest of the human figures (Pl. 1, scene 5; Pl. 2, scene 7).

The most dramatic change in the paintings is the concern for anatomical accuracy and detail in some of the human and animal forms (Fig. 38).[31] Coupled with the new-found tendency towards naturalism is the interest in depicting figures in a wide variety of poses (Fig. 39). The narrative role played by clothing in the early paintings has, in the renderings of Big Swan (Pl. 1, scenes 2a–d), given way to a more decorative approach. Some of the images draw from a much more extensive colour palette than is found in the early paintings. The paintings of Big Swan and Leans Over Butchering were executed with European painting implements, facilitating greater detail and size diminution (Pl. 1, scenes 2a–d, 5).

Also apparent in the Morris paintings is a greater sense of movement. This was achieved by combining profile views, which "are associated with speed and direction" (Deregowski 1984:115), with a wide variety of animated poses (Figs. 40–41). Full-profile views of humans seem to have been absent from the early Blackfoot paintings (Rodee 1965:222). Also in contrast to the early robes were depictions of horses with legs outstretched, at a flying gallop (Pl. 1, scene 2b; Pl. 2, scenes 6, 12).

In the preceding discussion about visual aspects of Blackfoot pictography it is readily apparent that the painters of the Morris robes approached their task in a relatively conservative manner, preserving many traditional pictorial conventions. In part, this may be connected to Morris' intervention and his desire to acquire examples of traditional-style picture-writing. The painters show considerable variation in individual style while working within the traditional framework. At the same time, certain aspects of the visual vocabulary employed on the Morris robes suggest significant change.

Traditional Blackfoot pictography and 19th-century European painting may be differentiated by two distinct pictorial systems. European artists tended to replicate the act of seeing by recreating scenes as perceived by the eye, while Blackfoot painters tended to produce conceptual images (Grinnell 1892:249; Dunn 1968:30–31; Petersen 1971:56) by constructing scenes through mental processes. European painters endeavoured to imitate three-dimensional space, while the Blackfoot conceived of pictorial space as strictly two-dimensional. Perceptual psychologists use the term *eidolic* (Deregowski 1984:20),[32] from the Greek word for phantom, to describe the kind of images produced by European painters. In contrast, they define the type of image produced by the traditional Blackfoot war painters as *epitomic*, a term derived from the Greek word for epitomize. The different sets of pictorial conventions employed by European and Blackfoot painters give rise to the notion of two distinct visual systems, one oriented towards epitomic images and the other towards eidolic images.

It is apparent that many pictorial conventions associated with the European system do not dovetail easily with their counterparts in the Blackfoot system. Forms cannot be highly abstracted and anatomically accurate at the same time. The potential for integration either of three-dimension-

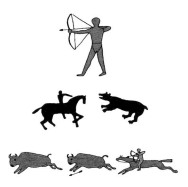

Figure 38 The anatomical features are accurately depicted in these figures, with the one exception in the position of the archer. The torso is displayed frontally, while the lower body is rotated ninety degrees and shown in profile, reflecting the earlier manner of rendering the human form. From Running Rabbit's robe (Pl. 2, scenes 4, 11–12).

Figure 39 Although this scene painted by Big Swan is stylistically worlds apart from Bull Plume's battle scene (Fig. 30), it depicts a similar if not identical event. It is unlikely that such a large portion of Sioux would be wearing flared war bonnets, particularly since such headdresses did not come into popular use until the 1890s (Howard 1954). From the robe of the Four Peigan Chiefs (Pl. 1, scene 2a).

Figure 40 Four events by Running Wolf with full-profile views and animated poses of people show European influence while creating a sense of action and movement. From the robe of the Four Peigan Chiefs (Pl. 1, scenes 1g, 1j).

Figure 41 Horses running with necks outstretched, riders with their whips and hair flying back, flying bullets, and running figures combine to heighten the action as a Cree war party attacks the Sarcee. From Bull Head's robe (Pl. 4, scene 3).

al and two-dimensional systems, or of diachronic and synchronic scenes, is limited. The intermixing of single-point perspective with a system of multiple vantage points is problematical. In the eidolic system there is a tendency to include all details within the field of vision, whereas the epitomic system tends to exclude all but the essential details. Considerable give and take is required in order to use both systems within the same picture frame.

The artists of the Morris robes did, nevertheless, bring both systems into play, reflecting the draughtsmen as active warriors in the years 1850–77, along with their adaptation to a Euro-Canadian–dominated society after settling on reserves. In one sense, the relationship implicit in the term *picture-writing* aptly describes the combination of the two visual systems. With respect to pictorial art, the Blackfoot's transition into the 20th century was marked by an increasing emphasis not on the literate but on the pictorial side of the equation. In part, this may have been due to a shift from one viewing audience to another. The earlier works were seen principally by Blackfoot, and there were numerous cultural events in which the content of the pictures received detailed elaboration through mime and the spoken word. The later paintings were intended for a European audience not privy to such occasions. As such, the later paintings may have become more "realistic" and self-explanatory, partly in accord with the demands of a new viewer group that lacked the means to readily appreciate the subject matter.[33]

DOCUMENTATION OF THE
MORRIS ROBES

Perhaps the most interesting observation that emerges from a visual analysis of the Morris robes is the incongruity between the two approaches to image making. In order to gain a greater understanding of why some of the artists chose to combine the two approaches, we turn to the rich documentation associated with the Morris robes.

Several images on the robes are apparently the work of younger artists. The large archer, the bear hunter, and the mounted buffalo hunter on Running Rabbit's robe (Pl. 2, scenes 4, 11–12) are almost certainly the work of his son, White Man. Among Morris' archival papers there are two pencil drawings by White Man of a "Mexican" saddle and a painted ceremonial tipi (Fig. 42).[34] Both drawings are carefully modelled and foreshortened to produce volume and detail, in the manner of European draughtsmanship. Interestingly, Morris referred to White Man as an "artist," whereas he termed those who painted the robes "tribal recorders." Similarly, the first events on Calf Child's robe (Pl. 5, scenes 1–3), which were painted by his son Joe,[35] presumably the only other young collaborator on the Morris robes, also tend towards realistic depiction, including such details as saddles. While boys grew up on reserves looking with great interest to the rapidly expanding array of non-native culture, they also listened intently as their fathers and grandfathers told them of horse raids and war parties from the past (Fig. 43).[36] The narrators evoked vivid mental images, which their young listeners then vicariously experienced by tracing them out in realistic graphic forms.[37]

The forces that shaped the older chiefs' style of depiction were of a different nature. The documentation associated with Chief Running Rabbit is an indication of the role of the Canadian government and its policy of rewarding native leaders who assimilated the ways of the white man while depriving those who held on to their traditions (Goldfrank 1945:71). In a photograph taken by Morris in 1907 (Fig. 44), Running Rabbit holds a cane given on behalf of Queen Victoria in 1890, when the federal government appointed him head chief of the Siksika (Morris 1985:18). He wears an official coat and a large medal that were presented by the Dominion of Canada in recog-

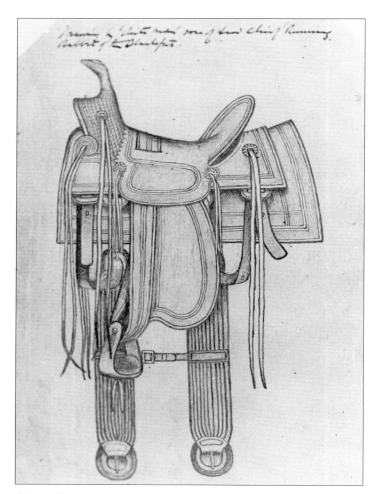

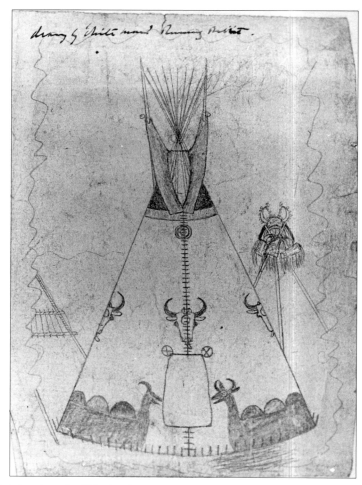

Figure 42 White Man, son of Running Rabbit, drew this carefully modelled drawing of a "Mexican" saddle, which probably represents one of the objects most highly coveted by young Blackfoot men in the early 20th century. Painted tipis were owned by only a few important individuals in Blackfoot society. When ownership changed, the painted designs were ritually transferred and the new owner was required to learn the songs and rules associated with the tipi. White Man's tipi drawing incorporates the conventional design of a buffalo head with protruding tongue. Courtesy Provincial Archives of Manitoba, Winnipeg.

nition of his signing Treaty No. 7. Several other medals are pinned to his coat.[38] These kinds of insignia became familiar to the Blackfoot about 1760 when the Hudson's Bay Company "made it a matter of policy to deal only with chiefs and headmen and had conferred honours upon them (medals, chiefs' coats, etc.) to enhance their authority over their followers" (Lewis 1942:42). Such honorific items were highly valued because the Blackfoot traditionally placed great significance on elaborate customs and heraldic insignia relating to prestige and power (Ewers 1939:17; Wissler 1911:37). Considering Running Rabbit's words in a letter to Morris dated 24 January 1909 however, the honours conferred upon him rang hollow: "We are pretty hungry this winter. We have no rations and only our work to live on. All are working very hard in the coal mines. I have a pipe bag and a pair of moccasins I could sell."[39]

The documentation associated with several other Blackfoot leaders elaborates on the assimilation of Euro-Canadian symbols by traditional native culture. For instance, on the robe of the Four Peigan Chiefs (Pl. 2, scene 1a), Running Wolf recalls an event that occurred around 1870:

> Big tent of a chief Nez Percés . . . Crowd of Nez Percés and Snake Indians in around: I was young then: Trusting in the medal of a great White Chief (around my neck) one evening I managed to reach the teepee and I rushed in. The Indians then yelled and made for me . . . Then I seized a young Child of the Chief and clasped him on my bosom: The chief Nez Percé changed his mind then: He says: "He is no more my enemy; he is in my teepee, he is under my protection; Don't touch him!" So I was saved.[40]

The protective powers that Running Wolf attributed to the medal[41] were essentially the same as those Calf Child attributed to his traditional war medicine, which consisted of the war bonnet of buffalo horns and ermine skins and the ceremonial shield shown on his robe (Pl. 5, scenes 1–3).[42]

The transfer of symbols of power from one culture to another is found in a wider context. At the time Morris commissioned the robes, the Canadian government was cutting food rations to pressure the Peigan and Siksika into selling parts of their reserves (Hanks and Hanks 1950:46). A large farm program was about to be implemented, which, coupled with the recent introduction of money, tended to undermine the horse as the traditional measure of wealth in Blackfoot economy (Goldfrank 1945:31). Blackfoot leaders, whose

Figure 43 The younger generation of Blackfoot are represented here by Willie White Pup (right), the son of Chief White Pup, and a friend. Photograph by Edmund Morris, 1907–10. Courtesy Provincial Archives of Manitoba, Winnipeg, Edmund Morris Collection 569.

Figure 44 Chief Running Rabbit and his son Houghton. The moccasins shown on Houghton are now in the Edmund Morris Collection of the Royal Ontario Museum (HK568). Photograph by Edmund Morris, 1907. Courtesy Provincial Archives of Manitoba, Winnipeg, Edmund Morris Collection 551.

power rested in their herds of horses and their ability to provide for their people, felt threatened (Goldfrank 1945:63; Kidd 1986:138). Bull Plume told of his fear of losing his chieftainship and of having to sell his horses to acquire food.[43] Leans Over Butchering expressed a similar fear to Father Doucet, who wrote of it to Morris:

> Chief Butcher . . . is afraid that the Department will do away shortly with him and the other Chiefs, and will take from them their chieftainship. He requests me to tell you that he likes to get some thing nice, not properly a medal but some-thing to show, some badge of some kind, to wear on his breast, something that shows nicely.[44]

Several other chiefs,[45] including Running Rabbit[46] and Running Wolf (Morris 1985:48), expressed a similar sense of helplessness and asked Morris to use his influence with the government to consolidate their political positions and stop the sale of reserve land.[47]

In exchange for painting their histories the four Peigan chiefs asked Morris for rings, medals, a telescope, official-looking coats, and canes, as well as flags to hoist over the "house on Sundays and feast days."[48] Significantly, the war-exploit robe, a symbol of power and prestige in traditional native culture, was now used to acquire objects that symbolized power and prestige in European culture. In the same way, it may be that the four Peigan chiefs willingly painted their exploits on the robe supplied by Morris because they knew it was destined to be exhibited in the Ontario Legislature. Doucet wrote to Morris:

> The Indians are proud to know that their painted buffalo robe has been admired by the white people and will remain for long time in the big house of the great Chiefs—it will encourage their research of curious articles for you.[49]

A month later Doucet noted in another letter to Morris that Leans Over Butchering was

> especially well pleased to know that their portraits will be in the great council house. I told him to tell all the other influential men about all that and to urge them to look for and collect old curious Indian articles of various kinds.[50]

Morris wanted Bull Plume, who was "the recorder of the tribe" (Morris 1909:15) and "the best to paint on skins,"[51] to paint the deeds of all four chiefs.[52] Bull Plume agreed, although his first response was that he would rather "paint on a story paper in book form."[53] However, it appears that Leans Over Butchering, Big Swan, and Running Wolf insisted on painting their own exploits on the robe. In light of their understanding that the robe was to be displayed in the Ontario legislative building, it is possible that the three chiefs participated in the painting of the robe with a view to consolidating their political positions in the eyes of the government.[54] Predictably, they were at odds with Bull Plume during the entire realization of the robe and even questioned the veracity of his accounts.[55] Big Swan and Running Wolf wrote their initials to identify themselves on the robe, and Butcher wrote out his name in full, but Bull Plume maintained a more traditional position by not identifying himself in his painted exploits (See Fig. 45). He believed that "the ways of the white race are not for Indians" (Morris 1909:15). On the other hand, the other chiefs were known as friendly to the white man[56] and were more likely to want to curry favour with the government. While Indians generally viewed Morris as sympathetic to their old ways, they must also have associated him with the government—in light of his connections with the Department of Indian Affairs, his contracts with provincial governments, and his father's pivotal role in the treaty negotiations. In this context, Bull Plume may have maintained his traditional painting style because he perceived Morris as championing traditional Indian ways. In contrast, the other Peigan chiefs may have viewed Morris as an arm of the government. This being the case, it is interesting to consider that the three chiefs' European style of depiction may have been in part influenced by their observation that the government rewarded Indian leaders who conformed to European values and forms.

The documentation does suggest, after all, that government pressure felt by the Blackfoot—both to give up much of their traditional way of life and to sell their reserve lands—left an imprint on the Morris robes. In broader terms, it might be said that the fundamental differences between native and non-native political, economic, and religious interests are reflected in the two visual systems. The combination of the two incongruous visual systems in Blackfoot pictorial art of the early 1900s may thus serve as a metaphor for the profound and unsettling changes to which the culture was forced to adjust.

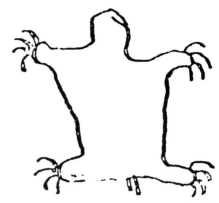

Figure 45 Name glyphs were the traditional means of identifying individuals in Plains Indian paintings and drawings. In the Glenbow Archives there is a list of more than a hundred individuals with corresponding name glyphs drawn by Bull Plume. Reproduced here is Bull Plume's pictographic representation of Edmund Morris' Blackfoot name, Bear Robe. It was drawn on a letter from Father Léon Doucet to Morris, 17 March 1909 (Morris Papers). Courtesy Provincial Archives of Manitoba, Winnipeg.

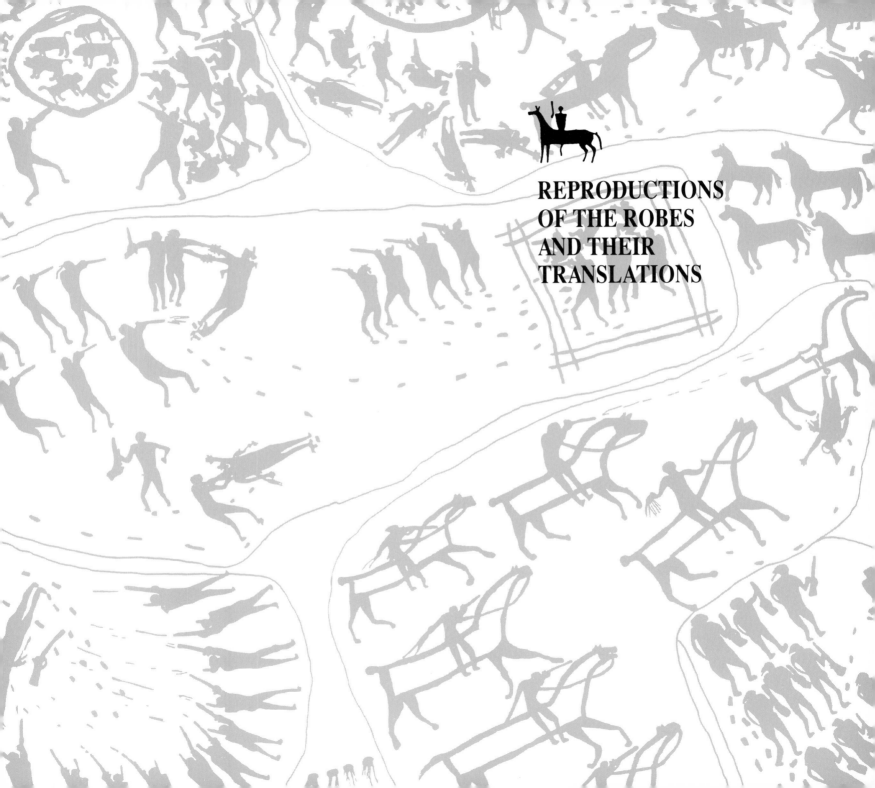

REPRODUCTIONS
OF THE ROBES
AND THEIR
TRANSLATIONS

A NOTE ON THE ENGLISH TEXTS

Before exposure to the European system of writing, the Blackfoot, like all aboriginal Plains peoples, passed on their traditions and history almost exclusively through the spoken word. When Edmund Morris commissioned written accounts of the events inscribed on his robes, however, rather than attempting to preserve a record of the brave deeds as they would have been recited in a traditional context, he sought to "translate the picture-writing." It is perhaps for this reason that some of the translations are so brief, as if to reflect the visual shorthand of the pictographs.

The variation in the length of the texts may be a reflection of the various translators rather than of the histories themselves. The text pertaining to the robes of Running Rabbit and Wolf Carrier are remarkable for their brevity. In a photograph Morris took of the work in progress we see Running Rabbit's son Houghton taking notes in English as his father describes his war exploits in Blackfoot (Fig. 5). Wolf Carrier's words were translated from Blackfoot into English by Mike Running Wolf and Sam Red Old Man (Morris 1985:158). The translators of these robes may have been limited in their writing skills and their fluency in English. On the other hand, the texts of the three remaining translators, Doucet, Erasmus, and the unnamed interpreter of Bull Head's narration, are fairly lengthy. Father Léon Doucet, whose mother tongue was French, wrote out the translation of the robe of the Four Peigan Chiefs while the chiefs explained their war deeds in Blackfoot.[57] Peter Erasmus, who was of Cree and Danish descent, translated the text for Calf Child's robe. Calf Child, who spoke both Cree and Blackfoot, described his war deeds in Cree to Erasmus, who then interpreted for Morris in English (Morris 1985:104). Erasmus and Doucet both tended to be wordy in their letters to Morris. The fifth robe was left with George Hodgson, the government interpreter on the Sarcee reserve, to arrange for the recording of Bull Head's war history. Two Guns, the "tribal recorder," did the actual painting and Hodgson's daughter Katherine wrote down the text. Bull Head narrated the events in the Sarcee language to an interpreter hired by Katherine.[58]

The length and elaboration found in the texts of the non-native translators may have been partly due to their greater command of the English language and their familiarity with European literary traditions. In any case, the translations before us are quite different from the traditional oral accounts which would have been very detailed and accompanied by mime, gesture, intonation, and even music.

The transcriptions below contain some peculiarities that should be noted. Dashes and ellipsis points that appear in the original transcriptions have been reproduced here; they do not indicate missing text except where noted. Spelling and punctuation have been reproduced as faithfully as possible from the original (see Fig. 46). At times portions of the histories were translated and transcribed in the third person rather than the first.

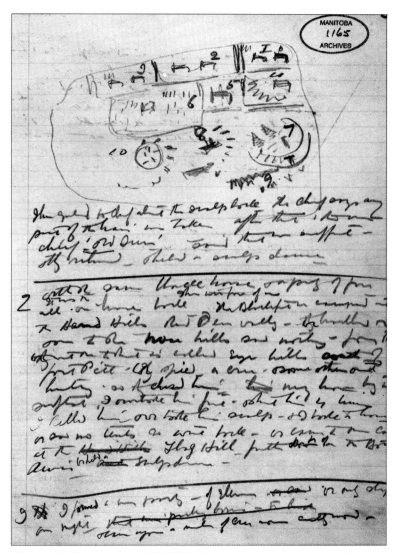

Figure 46 Transcription of Calf Child's war exploits as painted on his robe. The numbered paragraphs are keyed to the numbered scenes on the robe. From the diary of Edmund Morris, 1907–9, first draft, p. 85. Courtesy Provincial Archives of Manitoba, Winnipeg.

PLATE 1. THE ROBE OF THE FOUR PEIGAN CHIEFS

178 cm × 183 cm
Royal Ontario Museum HK461

This robe was painted by four chiefs: Running Wolf, Big Swan, Bull Plume, and Leans Over Butchering. The painting was completed not long before 17 March 1909, when Father Léon Doucet met with the four chiefs to transcribe their narrations.

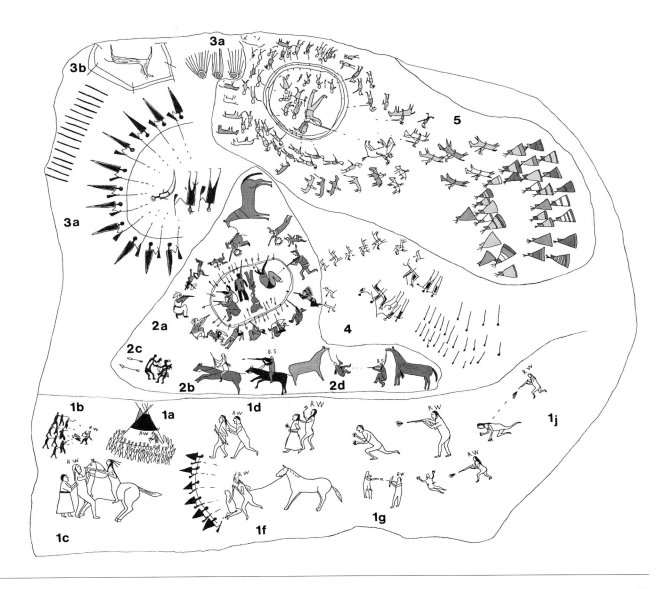

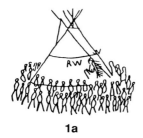

1a

1b

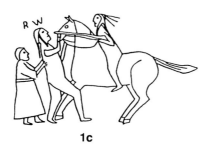

1c

1d

The Robe of the Four Peigan Chiefs

The following transcription is taken directly from a letter from Father Léon Doucet to Edmund Morris, 17 March 1909 (Morris Papers).

Running Wolf

[1a] Big tent of a chief Nez Percés . . . Crowd of Nez Percés and Snake Indians in around: I was young then: Trusting in the medal of a great White Chief (around my neck) one evening I managed to reach the teepee and I rushed in. The Indians then yelled and made for me . . . Then I seized a young Child of the Chief and clasped him on my bosom: The chief Nez Percé changed his mind then: He says: "He is no more my enemy; he is in my teepee, he is under my protection; Don't touch him!" So I was saved—I have been on the Warpath very many times.

[1b] Two of us were attacked by a party of Gros Ventres . . . My friend was killed. I killed one and took his revolver.

[1c] Many Kootenay attacked us: They took all I had; but I managed to go away and to have one woman, a cousin of mine.

[1d] Gros Ventres again. I killed one and took his scalp.
   At Cypress Hill . . . Fight the Crees . . . I spared one Cree, but another Peigan killed him.

[1f] At Cypress Hill . . . Fight with a party of Gros Ventres. I spared, a Woman, but another killed her—I was leading my horse, and I killed one man (Gros Ventre). Kneeling—

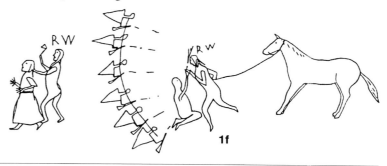

1f

[1g] On the War path against the River Crow (Net-artes[?] tappi)—with bow and arrows—I could ride—my horse was plaid out. In the fight, I shot three (with arrows).

At Cypress Hills . . . My war party attacked a big camp of Crees and prairie Assiniboines. Surprise of the enemies . . . Panic. It was a running fight . . . About seventy teepees of the enemies, they run away, we take their teepees and all their belongings. We were a good number.

We held a big Sun Dance at Cypress Hill long ago . . . Attacked by Crees or Assiniboines—I killed one in the Hills.

[1j] We had a big fight with the Crows or some other Indians far South. Many of both sides. I killed one enemy. I don't know exactly who were these Southern Indians.

Big Swan

[2a] It was in the Winter—I was with some Peigans on the War path Cross the Missouri. We were surprised and attacked by a big party of Sioux . . . We fought the whole day—from early morning to night. Two of us were killed . . . There was one woman the wife of one of us . . . At night we managed to escape. I am painted with the green jacket. The Sioux had guns and bows— We killed four Sioux—

1g

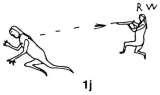

1j

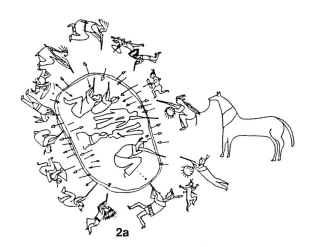

2a

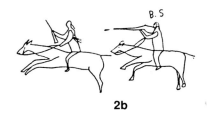

2b

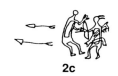

2c

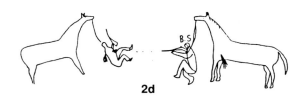

2d

[2b] I killed one Gros Ventres and took his gun.

[2c] One Gros Ventre shoots me with arrow. I take his bow and kill him.

[2d] The Horse painting red . . . Great fight between the Kootenays and the Peigans . . . One Kootenay shoots my horse, I kill him. Another Peigan or a Blood takes the horse and gun. Many Bloods Indians were on the War path with the Peigans—I had many fights mostly in Cypress Hills' country, against northern and southern Indians.

Bull Plume

[3a] The three scalp red—35 years ago . . . fight with Prairie Assiniboines— Two were killed by a Blood Indian—one by a Peigan. I got the 3 scalps. — The fight, We were attacked by a great number of Sioux, camped in the bush . . . We did not see them they attacked us . . . the whole day . . . —7 Indians escaped before the fight . . . 6 of us had to fight. Two got killed (of us) . . . About dusk we managed to escape from the Sioux.

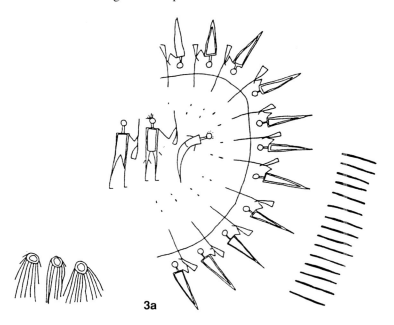

3a

[3b] Another fight . . . at Cypress Hills: I was about 18 years of age . . . There was a Cree Teepee, and a fine white horse tied in a kind of corral close by. I untied the horse, and made away with him . . . I was shot by the Crees in the Teepees—They didn't touch me . . . I shot two and I killed one Cree— as I learned afterwards.

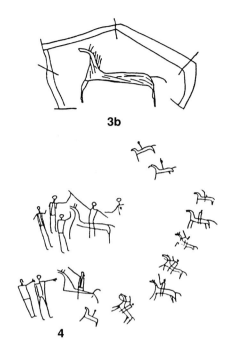

3b

[4] He [Bull Plume] is [on] horseback going to the Kootenay camp, against the advice of Old Eagle Tail—Peigan Chief—There was a little before a fight . . . and a few has been killed of both sides . . . Three Kootenay Indians jumped on me—they threw me from my horse, and they were to kill me, but the Kootenay Chief rushed and saved my life . . . the man a little behind me is Chief Butcher . . . He was unhurt too.

Leans Over Butchering

[5] I was on a warpath far in Montana—near a place called "Owl's Head" . . . We met a very large camp of Sioux Indians.

We were 13 of us . . . From morning to night they tried to force us from our light entrenchment.

My companions were all killed—and I managed some how to escape through the night . . . You see the teepees . . . that is the Sioux camp . . . a very large one.[59]

4

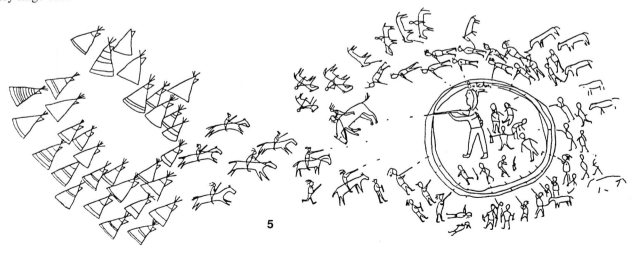

5

PLATE 2. RUNNING RABBIT'S ROBE

170 cm × 190 cm
Royal Ontario Museum HD6541

The figures on this robe are colour coded; the Cree are in red, the Crow in yellow, and the Blackfoot in blue or black. The robe was painted and translated in August 1909.

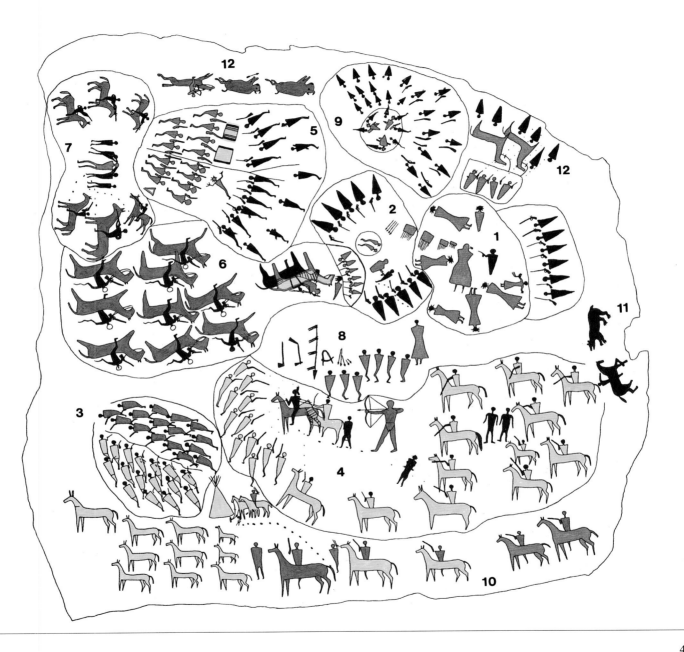

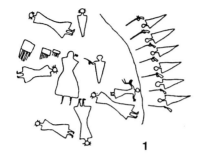

1

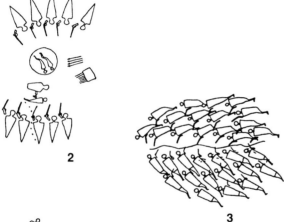

2

3

Running Rabbit's Robe

The following transcription is from *The Diaries of Edmund Montague Morris: Western Journeys 1907–1910* (Morris 1985:92).

1. When I was 17 I joined a war party against the Crees. We came on a camp. The men were all off after the buffalo. We killed all the women except one young girl whom I took captive.

2. Join with a war party into the Cree country. We sighted the enemy who entrenched themselves in a hole in the ground. I killed one of them & took his scalp.

3. A large war party went to the Crows. A big fight followed. We killed a lot of them.

4. Again in the Crow country we are surrounded by a large number. They killed one of the Bloods. My horse was wounded. I jumped on another but got a wound from an arrow before I got away.

5. We fall in with the Crees—a big fight. The Crees held up blankets suing for peace.

4

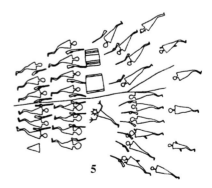

5

6. Again met the Crees. We drove them into a lake. They had difficulty running through the mud & we killed them all.

7. Again met the Crees. I killed the chief Handsome Young Man.

8. Represents the Crees he killed—a spear, war pipe, & war club, & powder flask taken from the Crows.

9. An encounter with the Crees.

10. Horses he took from the Crows.

11. He killed four grizzly bear.

12. The buffalo hunt. Hunts out Crees who had stolen 4 horses, he took them all back.

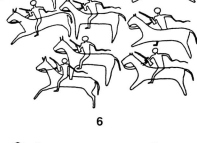

6

7

8

9

10

11

12

PLATE 3. WOLF CARRIER'S ROBE

154 cm × 174 cm
Royal Ontario Museum HK457

This robe was painted in 1909 or 1910 and translated in October 1910.

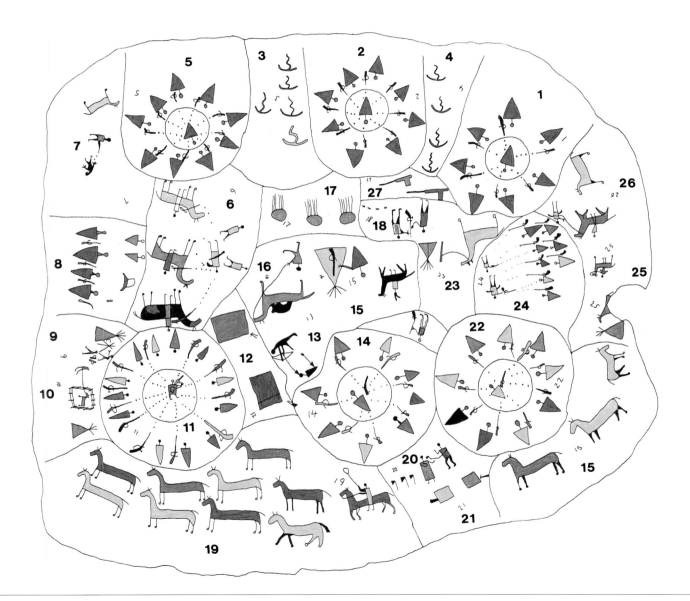

51

1

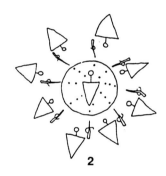

2

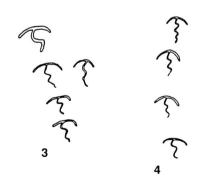

3

4

Wolf Carrier's Robe

The following transcription is from *The Diaries of Edmund Montague Morris: Western Journeys 1907–1910* (Morris 1985:158–59).

1. 3 Blackfoot in a coulee around which they had placed rocks. Pretty Young Man was the leader. They had gone to the Crow country to steal horses. Wolf Carrier was still a boy but had gone with them.

2. The Blackfoot went to the Cypress Hills to steal horses from the Assiniboines.

Before they reached the camp they came on a large gather of Assiniboines, Gros Ventres & Crows—at a Sun Dance. They turned on the Blackfoot & killed 6 of them—then let the others escape. Big Beaver was leader of that war party of the Blackfoot—it happened about 47 years ago.

3–4. Wolf Carrier had been an Indian scout, these record the number of times he sighted the enemy.

5. Two sons of an old Blackfoot had been killed & to revenge this a large war party of Bloods & Blackfoot numbering over 100. They followed the Bow River down—& on to the camp of the Assiniboines & Crees. They came on the camp & hid in the bushes till morning. It was winter. They attacked but were outnumbered & 50 of the braves were killed, the rest retreated.

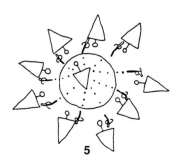

5

6. Flat Heads had stolen Blackfoot horses. They went after them—& took horses. They were followed & a fight took place.

7. A Cree he killed, & a horse he took from a Flat Head.

8. While sleeping—the Flat Heads came upon them—2 killed. They took a powder horn.

9. He crept on the Flat Head camp & killed 2 men, 2 women & 4 kids. It was in the daytime.

10. He crossed the mountains & found some Indians—at night captured a horse.

11. 40 Blackfoot went against the Crows, to steal horses. Weasel Tail was the leader. Near the Missouri the Crows outnumbered them & drove them out of a coulee—killing a number of them—a head man & Wolf Flat Head amongst them.

12. Buffalo robes taken from the Crow Indians. His hands are represented.

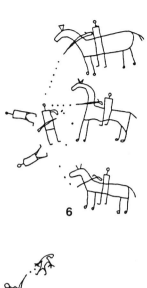

6

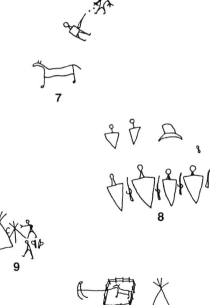

7

8

9

10

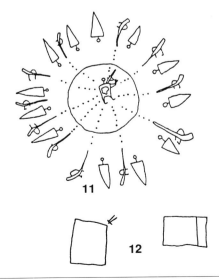

11

12

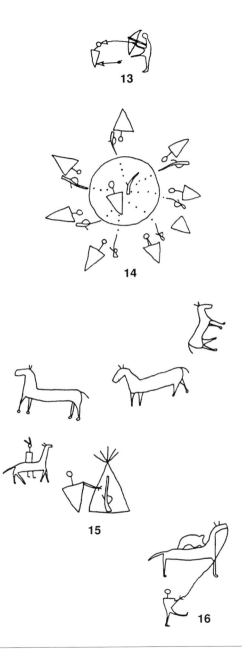

13. They are again after the Crees. Wolf Carrier got wounded—an arrow went through his cheek & another through his foot.

14. Eagle Chief led a party of Blackfoot against the Crows. They fought from a coulee.

15. A Flat Head lodge. He took a gun & 2 buckskin horses & 2 sorrel horses.

16. Took a Flat Head horse & mounted it.

17. Cree scalps of women. He killed them because they were ugly.

18. A chief of Crees called "Wood". Fought him & took his gun—he says the Cree cried, so he did not kill him.[60]

19. He got 9 horses from the Flat Heads—the same time.

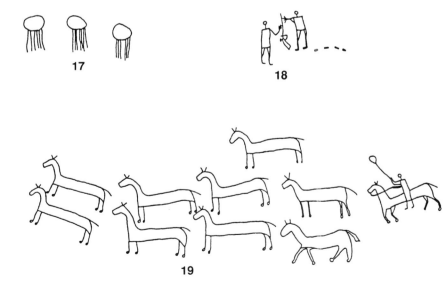

20. Killed a Cree woman & took 4 ——— [illegible word].

21. Crow robes he stole.

22. Again to the Crows & at night, tried to take horses. The Crows hid & fought them & drove them away.

23. A horse stolen from Flat Heads.

24. Blackfoot against the Crows. He & another scout out ahead—came on a large camp. The other scout got killed.

25. Took 2 Flat Head horses.

26. Took horse of Crow Indian. He is on it, then off.

27. Crow pipes.

20

21

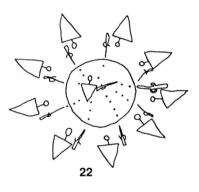

22

23

24

25

26

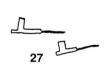

27

PLATE 4. BULL HEAD'S ROBE

200 cm × 220 cm
Royal Ontario Museum HK459

The figures on this robe are colour coded; the Cree are in blue or black and the Sarcee in green or red. Morris brought this robe to the Sarcee in the summer of 1908 and the painting was completed in November of the same year. Bull Head's war history was painted by Two Guns, the "tribal recorder." A

letter to Morris dated 18 November 1908 from Katherine Hodgson, who transcribed the translation of the robe, reveals that Morris paid twenty dollars to have the robe painted, ten dollars going to Bull Head for giving information (Morris Papers).

Bull Head's Robe

The following translation was written down by Katherine Hodgson and included in a letter from Elizabeth Hodgson to Edmund Morris, 3 December 1908 (Morris Papers).

1. In the year 1860, at Nose Hill about 100 miles East of Edmonton, as Crees were engaged in building a fort, when all unexpectedly a Sarcee War party came upon them, in which chief Little Chief was leader.

The Sarcees immediately attacked the Crees. A fight followed lasting a few hours. One of the Crees, bolder than the rest, rushed out of the fort carrying a Holy Item and a gun. He was shot in one foot by Many Horses. Blood also fired at him. He made an attempt to escape but Bulls Head shot and afterwards scalped him, taking the scalp and gun.

2. In the same year 1860, one winter day, at Battle River near Dried Meat Lake, the Sarcees had driven a large band of Buffaloes into a "Buffalo Pawn" [pound]. (A Buffalo Pawn [pound] is an enclosure built of logs. Built by the Indians for capturing the Buffalo.) And while butchering the animals they had just killed, aided by the women and children a party of Crees surprised them. In an instant they were prepared for fight. Many managed to reach the camp, which was near by, Bulls Head who had reached his tepee, shot and killed one of the enemy.

The Crees were defeated and fled. Four of the Sarcee braves were killed.

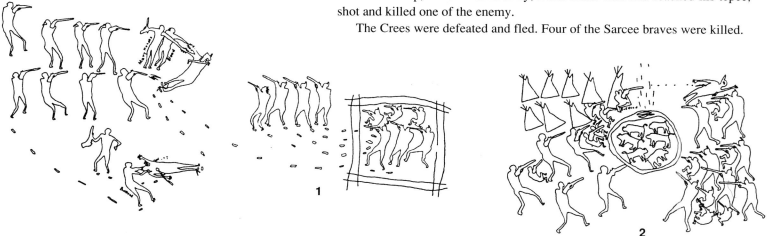

58

3. In the month of May 1865, one bright morning, "Riding on the Side Hill" started off alone to hunt, intending to return that day, but next day when he had not returned his friends became alarmed and the chief Little Chief (Bull's Head's brother) ordered a party of men and women to go and search for him.

Some of the men were on foot and when they were some fifteen miles from camp they saw a man standing on a high hill, waving his blanket. Thinking he was their lost comrade they began to ascend the hill, but they were mistaken for this man was an enemy signalling to the Crees who were on the other side of the hill. When they discovered this they turned and fled, with the enemy in hot pursuit.

During the chase one of the Sarcee women fell off her horse and her husband who was too frightened to turn back called to Bull's Head to save her. He without hesitating turned and leaping from his horse aided her to mount hers. Many men were killed and seven women captured by the Crees.

Little Chief who had run all the way was shot and instantly killed on reaching their camp.

"Eagle rib" had everything in preparation in camp having heard the reports knew that they were in danger.

Bull's Head who had arrived in safety, upon hearing of his brothers death rushed out amongst the enemy followed by his wife and pulled one of them back into their enclosure by the hair. They cut his throat scalped him and took his gun.

This battle was fought at Vermillion Creek lasting all day and was one of the fiercest battles fought amongst the Indians' tribes.

The Sarcees had camped near a slough and after the battle it was like a pool of blood.

4. A few weeks after Little Chief was killed while the Sarcees were camping at Battle River some of their horses were stolen.

Suspecting where the horses were taken to Bull's Head gathered a few men and rode away.

They soon came upon a party of Crees building a fort. One of the Crees came to meet them asking to be friends, but Bull's Head who had not forgotten his brother's death jumped from his horse and sprang at the Cree with the intention of killing him but ended by only taking his gun and giving it to "Heaven Fire".

The others made no attempt to fight so they parted in peace.

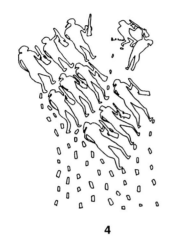

4

5. In the Summer of 1886 a party of Sarcees met a few Crees who seeing the Sarcees outnumbered them, fled.

The Sarcees killed nine of them and wounded one.

Bulls Head sprang from his horse and taking a knife from the wounded man stabbed him and took his scalp.

This took place at Long Lake.

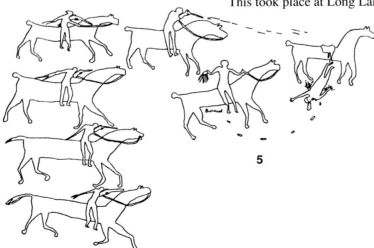

5

6. In 1866, a party of Sarcees made ready to go to Edmonton to trade. While on the way "Bull's Head", "Going to the Crees" and "Little Boy" who were following at a distance, hunting for game, thought they saw a wolf on a hill and decide to try and killed it. As they approached near Bull's Head hesitated, telling his companions that he thought the object on the hill was a man and not a wolf, but they would not believe him and finally persuaded him to follow.

When they reached the summit they not only saw one man but a number of Crees who instantly fired at them.

Bull's Head who was so taken by surprise could not run. He walked a few steps then the fright seemed to leave him and running he soon joined his companions who had reached the bottom of the hill again. The main party of Sarcees hearing the firing fled also. Little Boy arrow case was shot off his back, but he was not hurt. "Going to the Crees" was killed.

After running five or six miles with the enemy following close firing all the time they were met by Bull's Head's wife with two horses. Then the two men mounted one horse and they soon outran their pursuers who were not mounted.

The five horses that are painted on the side are the horses that Bulls Head had stolen from other tribes, also the Tomahawks, scalps and bows and arrows.[61]

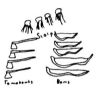

6

PLATE 5. CALF CHILD'S ROBE

150 cm × 188 cm
Royal Ontario Museum HK469

This robe was painted and translated in August 1909. When Morris was almost finished transcribing the events on the robe Calf Child's wife called out, "He's not telling you half he did." Calf Child said of his wife that "she was brave & often came out [on the warpath] with me" (Morris 1985:106).

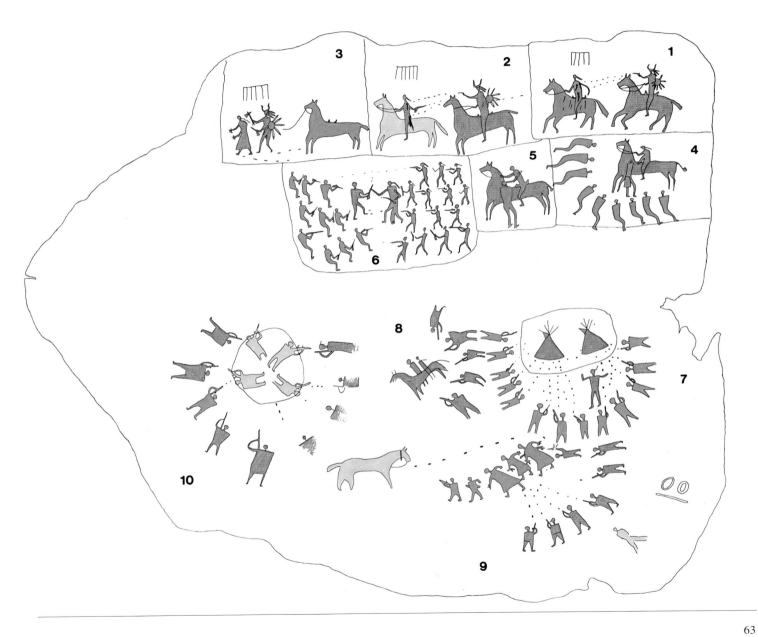

63

Calf Child's Robe

Most of the following transcription is taken from the second draft of Morris' diary (see Morris 1985:104) in the Royal Ontario Museum, but in some instances additional information was included from the first draft of the diary, pp. 85–89, in the Provincial Archives of Manitoba.

1. When young I started off with a war party. My father told me—my son you are a fine looking young man, don't spoil your good looks by being a coward. You have a fine horse. Mount him, take your war clothes with you, and try & be first. Above all, try & capture some horses & take a scalp. This is how a man proves himself to be brave.

We were coming near the country of the Crees. I was sent out as a scout with three others. We saw a Cree & forced on our horses. I came up to him first—I [had a six shooter & shot him three times] shot & killed him & took his scalp—the others took the rest. I took his horse.

2. We the Blackfoot are encamped at the Hand Hills, Red Deer Valley—a party of five of us. I had the same black horse. We went on to the Nose Hills but sighted none of the enemy and rode on to the Eye Hills south of Fort Pitt. Here we spied a Cree with others out hunting. We gave chase. My horse was the swiftest. I overtook him, shot him (four times) & took his scalp. We came back to our camp at Flag Hills further down, north of Battle River. Here we held a scalp dance. ——— ——— ——— ——— ——— ——— ———. [Illegible]

1

2

3. I formed a party of eleven for a raid. Starting off we rode night & day. We came upon a number of Cree women cutting wood & rushed on them. I was ahead and, as I came up to them, jumped off my horse & led it. One of the women struck out at me with her axe. I guarded the blow but got wounded in the head. I got hold of the axe & smashed her head in. Shots were exchanged, & hearing it the Crees came rushing down from camp. We rode off. I was forming a rearguard & called out for them not to go, so we turned back & had an encounter—& the Crees fled.[62]

3

4. We started off a war party—a great number. We met the Crees at the Eye Hills, many of them. We fought—our party was to the south & the Crees to the north. We made a fort out of branches & the Crees came at us in it. I now had a large Bay horse, a swift mare, and getting restless rushed out naked & mounted my horse. One man came out to meet me. I ran against him with my horse & knocked him down & took his gun & quiver of arrows but did not kill him. The Crees all firing at me. 2 of our party killed, & three Crees.

5. In the early morning, when at the Knee Hills in my lodge, my Sarcee woman called out, I think we are attacked by the Crees. I ran out naked as I was & jumped on my horse. The Crees had surrounded us. I got amongst them. A man came to meet me, he was on foot. I got ahold of his scalp & gun, took both & killed him on the spot. We killed eleven Crees, none of us killed. I had been counted brave before, but I was now named by the tribe one of the braves.

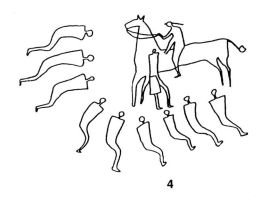

4

5

6

6. We are camped by a creek [near the Hand Hills]. The Flat Heads surprised us. Our scouts had been out but had seen nothing. The Flat Heads are all mounted. We chased them to another creek [somewhere near the Red Deer]. They jumped off their horses & left them & came on to fight us. We dismounted & met them. After a time they turned & fled. I overtook one (painted on robe red). He made to strike me with his gun but I shot him, took his guns & scalp—that ended the fight. The women all liked me for this!

7. At Battle River there are many, about 40, lodges of us camped east of Buffalo Lake. A war party of Crees—Big Bear, Little Pine, & Poundmaker, & their following came upon us at night. We had made a sort of fort of brush. Father Lacombe & John Lereux were in my tent, Lacombe spoke in Cree to them telling them to go away but they would not & he nearly got killed by a ball (bullet) passing through his black robe. It was a hard fight & lasted all night. I went outside the enclosure, fighting them, & my Sarcee woman stood within singing the war song. I had my war bonnet of buffalo horns & ermine skins.

I took 2 scalps. The fight lasted till daylight, then the Crees fled. 3 women and 2 men of our people killed. We counted 5 Crees killed. It was here my Sarcee woman got a bullet wound.[63]

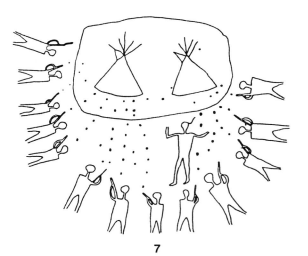

7

8. 12 Crees on a horse stealing expedition were observed near our camp. I jumped on my horse & chased them & got in amongst them. I ran against one of them & knocked him down. While I was fighting him a Cree from behind jumped on my horse to kill me, the others firing all the time. I held him & rode hard to camp & threw him down amongst the lodges & told the women to kill him. None of them—Poundmaker, Big Bear, Piapot—ever did this. I was now made war chief.

9. I took some of our party off. We spied 5 Crees sitting on the edge of a wood, three women & two men. I told my men to wait & I would go & see. I shot some of them, & my men coming up killed the others.

I captured the horses and took a buckskin horse with a red cloth around its neck and gave it to my Sarcee woman. She was glad.

10. Near the Cypress Hills we came on a party of Crees in a coulee. We attacked them—they were some of Piapot's band. We are Blackfoot, Blood & Peigan all together (I am to the right on robe). I killed a Cree and got a bullet wound through my chest.

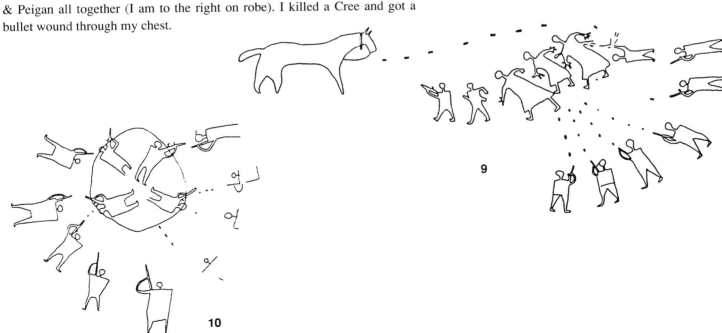

8

9

10

BIOGRAPHICAL NOTES

Running Wolf

Running Wolf, Apisomakau (Fig. 1), explained to ethnologist Walter McClintock that he was born in Montana, "in the year when white men were first seen in our country" (McClintock 1910:423; Paul Raczka, personal communication, 1993). According to tribal history, this would have been the year 1831.[64] He settled in Canada two years after the North West Mounted Police entered present-day Alberta, in 1876. He was the son of Iron Shirt, a former head chief of the Peigan. Iron Shirt, who died an old man, had survived three

sieges of smallpox. Running Wolf's grandfather, Sun Bull, was also an important chief. Running Wolf was chief of the Lone Fighters band. Father Doucet recalled in the early days Running Wolf's great tipi made of twenty-four buffalo skins and holding nineteen occupants. When visiting, Doucet slept in a room screened apart. After his days as a warrior ended, Running Wolf devoted his attentions to the religious and healing aspects of Blackfoot life (Raczka 1992:68). This shift was marked by his receiving a new name, Brings Down the Sun. He became the leader of the North Peigan Sun

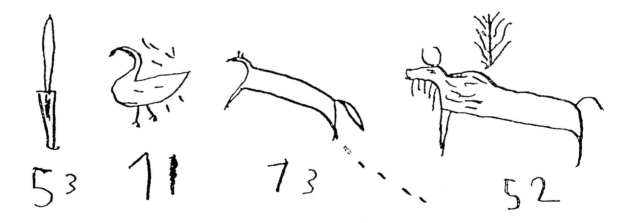

Figure 47 The name glyphs and ages of the four Peigan chiefs were inscribed by Bull Plume and included in a letter from Father Léon Doucet to Edmund Morris, 17 March 1909 (Morris Papers). From left to right: Leans Over Butchering, Big Swan, Running Wolf, and Bull Plume. In pictographic drawings, especially those of the Plains tribes south of the Blackfoot, a name glyph drawn above a human figure and connected to the head by a line was a common means of establishing identity. Courtesy Provincial Archives of Manitoba, Winnipeg.

Dance and custodian of the Pipe of Thunder Maker (Long Time Pipe), which was passed down from his father. He also became an expert on herbal medicine and was known as a peacemaker within the community. Running Wolf was very bitter about the attempts of non-natives to extinguish traditional native religion. Around 1905 his rations were cut off because he began making preparations to hold a Sun Dance. In 1908 Morris encountered him on his return from hunting eagles. He explained to Morris the arduous process of catching the birds and the prayers and rituals that followed their capture. He helped support his family by selling eagle feathers to the Montana Peigans for headdresses and other ceremonial materials (McClintock 1910:428–29). Brings Down the Sun and his wife, Bird, had thirteen children (McClintock 1910:532).

Big Swan

Big Swan, Akamakai, was born around 1855 (Fig. 2). He belonged to the Seldom Lonesome band and was a minor chief of the Peigan between 1877 and 1919. He was one of the participants in the signing of Treaty No. 7 in 1877.[65] At one time he owned a stopping house on the stagecoach line between Fort McLeod and Pincher Creek. Doucet noted that "Big Swan too was always friendly, he is more wealthy than Running Wolf, he was more industrious and smart to make money in the early times, but honest in his dealings." To this day people marvel at his wealth and the system of accounting that he developed without a formal, European education.[66] Big Swan died in 1920.

Bull Plume

Bull Plume, Stumiksisapo, was born a Siksika around 1856 and adopted at an early age by the Peigan (Fig. 3). Although Bull Plume was an orphan, he achieved considerable prominence in the North Peigan community. He was a minor chief from 1891 until 1919. His position in the tribe largely rested on his reputation as a ceremonialist and spiritual leader of traditional Blackfoot ways. Doucet noted in 1908 that Bull Plume was sponsoring a Sun Dance. McClintock (1910:387) was present when Bull Plume led the yearly ceremony for the renewal of the North Peigan medicine pipes around 1905.[67] Bull Plume was the last Peigan to keep up the tribal Winter Count, a record of tribal history maintained over a period of perhaps 150 years, each year marked by a pictograph representing an outstanding event. Doucet thought that Bull Plume was the person best informed on Blackfoot history and tradition (see Fig. 47).[68] Morris thought him to be the most interesting of the Peigan chiefs. He had a good intellect according to Morris (1909:15), who described Bull Plume as "of strong build," with a "voice like thunder," and with "movements . . . quick & restless as a panther." Bull Plume died in 1920.

Leans Over Butchering

Leans Over Butchering, Stokinota, also called Butcher or Chief Butcher, was born in Montana around 1855 (Fig. 4). As a boy his name was changed from Chief Straight Hair to Leans Over Butchering in recognition of one of his first acts of bravery. He was a survivor of a war party that was almost annihilated when it was ambushed by the Sioux. He received his name because he had the courage to check each Peigan victim to determine whether any of his fellow warriors were still alive before beginning his long journey home. He remained known as Leans Over Butchering and came into prominence as an active and accomplished warrior.[69] As an old man he took the name Black Plume. His father, Sitting on an Eagle Tail, was the head chief of the North

Peigans and signed Treaty No. 7 in 1877. Leans Over Butchering served as head chief between 1901 and 1921. Doucet described him as honest and friendly but poor and not very industrious. During his chieftainship he was remembered for his strong opposition to the Peigan land surrender of 1909.[70]

Running Rabbit

Running Rabbit, Atsistaumukkon, was born in 1833 (Fig. 5). When his brother died, in the mid-1870s, Running Rabbit replaced him as chief of the Biters band.[71] He earned a strong reputation for his kindness, his conciliatory skills, and his generosity in sharing the horses that he acquired through raiding. In 1892 he was named one of two head chiefs of the Blackfoot tribe. He was first called Last Medicine Man and later White Buffalo Lying Down before receiving the name Running Rabbit (Morris 1985:157). Running Rabbit gave Morris the Blackfoot name Kyaiyii, or Bear Robe, after a great Blackfoot chief. Running Rabbit worked hard farming his land. In 1898 he had his own wagon, mowing machine, and rake, and had made enough money cutting and selling hay to buy a high-top buggy.[72] Morris noted in 1909 (1985:111) that it was usual for Running Rabbit to rise at five in the morning to work in his garden. He had four wives and eleven children, one of which, Duck Chief, became head chief. Running Rabbit died in 1911.

Wolf Carrier

Morris apparently took no photographs of Wolf Carrier, nor did he make other than passing mention of him in his diaries. A photograph of Wolf Carrier taken in 1913 (Fig. 6) shows him as one of the dignitaries at a Sun Dance. He appears to be well into his seventies at the time.

Bull Head

Born in 1833, Bull Head, Stumixotocon, also known as Little Chief or Tçillah, was the most important Sarcee chief in recent memory (Fig. 7).[73] He was of mixed Blood/Sarcee ancestry (Morris 1985:24) and his wife was Blackfoot (Stocken 1976:26). They had two children, both of whom died young. Bull Head was "extremely tall, well over six feet two inches in his old age, and very broad shouldered . . . [with] a loud booming voice."[74] In 1877 he reluctantly signed Treaty No. 7 on behalf of his people. The Sarcee were initially placed on a reserve that abutted the Blackfoot reserve. The two tribes found it untenable to live in such close proximity, so Bull Head, through skilful bureaucratic strategy, acquired a reserve consisting of three townships of land immediately west of Calgary. Much of the chief's attention was directed towards solving social problems, especially prostitution and alcohol abuse, which stemmed partly from the closeness of Calgary. Starvation and disease among his people, particularly tuberculosis, were also constant concerns for Bull Head. To counteract these conditions the chief encouraged his people to be self sufficient by working their gardens, planting small plots of grain, and attending school. Hugh Dempsey has written that "perhaps Bull Head's greatest contributions were in keeping his people united and his reserve intact in spite of devastating social and health problems and the pressure of Calgarians who coveted their lands."[75] Bull Head served as chief of the Sarcee from 1865 until his death in 1911.

Calf Child

Calf Child, Onistaipoka, also called White Buffalo Calf and Lone Chief (his father's name), was a great war chief who had been in thirty-two inter-tribal fights (Fig. 8). He was head of the Black Soldiers and a member of the Strong Whips band. His father, Lone Chief, was a leader next to Crowfoot in stature. His wife was a Sarcee and the daughter of Chief White Buffalo Hoofs. Calf Child was also an eminent medicine man. Doucet remembered first seeing him at the deathbed of a chief: "He was masked & painted like a devil & blowing through bone tubes to drive out the evil spirits or sickness" (Morris 1985:46). Before he allowed Morris to paint his portrait, in order to determine whether it would be good for him to be painted, he consulted a wooden carving of the head of an old man with grey hair; it had a large mouth and eyes and was painted red (Morris 1985:101).[76] Morris described Calf Child as "one of the most intelligent & manly of the Blackfoot" he had encountered (1985:125) and noted that, although he was of advanced years, "his voice still rings like thunder when he invites his friends to his lodge" (1909:14).

APPENDIX

BLACKFOOT PICTOGRAPHS—COMPARATIVE EXAMPLES

Early Set

The thirteen paintings in the Early Set may be the only surviving Blackfoot war-exploit paintings on hide made exclusively for native use before settlement on reserves.

a. Undocumented Blackfoot robe, probably from the early 19th century (Musée de l'Homme, Paris, 96.73.1). Scholarly opinion seems to agree that this robe is Blackfoot (see Glenbow-Alberta Institute 1987:77; Vatter 1927:77). Illustrated in Vatter (1927, fig. 25) and Vitart (1993:101).

b. Blackfoot shirt collected in 1845 by Paul Kane (Manitoba Museum of Man and Nature, Winnipeg, H4.4.4). Illustrated in Taylor (1986:275).

c. Blood shirt collected by D'Otrante in Blackfoot territory, 1843–44 (Folkens Museum, Stockholm). Illustrated in Vatter (1927, fig. 27) and Brunius (1990:30).

d. Undocumented Blackfoot robe collected before 1861 (Nationalmuseet, Copenhagen, HC478). Scholarly opinion seems to agree that this robe is Blackfoot (Vatter 1927:77; Ewers 1983:54; Ted J. Brasser, personal communication, 1988). Illustrated in Vatter (1927, fig. 23) and Ewers (1983:57).

e. Drawing by Karl Bodmer of a Blackfoot warrior's robe entered in the journal of Prince Maximilian of Wied, 30 June 1833, vol. 2, pp. 154–55 (Josylin Museum of Art, Omaha). Illustrated in Thomas and Ronnefeldt (1976:17).

f. Drawing by Karl Bodmer, "Piegan Warrior,"1833 (Josylin Museum of Art, Omaha). Illustrated in Thomas and Ronnefeldt (1976:137).

g. Sketch by Paul Kane of the robe of Sinew Piece, a Blood, 1845 (Nelda C. and H. J. Lutcher Stark Foundation, Orange, Texas, WWC 82; CR-164). Illustrated in Harper (1971, fig. 95).

h. Photograph of a Blackfoot robe, taken by H. L. Hime in 1858 (Public Archives of Canada, Ottawa). Illustrated in Ewers (1945:22; 1983:56).

i. Blackfoot robe collected before 1898 (Royal Ontario Museum, Toronto, 975x73.6). Illustrated in Boyle (1904:55) and Maurer (1992:217). Although the documentation does not give information regarding the age of this robe, and it may have been executed after settlement on the reserve, I have included it in this set because the painting style and overall composition are identical to well-documented early robes.

j. Blackfoot shirt collected in 1842 (Pitt Rivers Museum, Oxford, 1893-67-1). Illustrated in Glenbow-Alberta Institute (1987:72).

k. Blackfoot shirt collected in the early 1800s (Brooklyn Museum, Brooklyn, 50.67.5a). Illustrated in Taylor (1986:276).

l. Undocumented Blackfoot robe, probably dating to around 1840 (National Museum of Ireland, Dublin, 1882:3881). "Said to have been acquired by one of

Captain Cook's companies on one of his voyages" (National Museum of Ireland, letter to the author, 28 February 1989). This robe was initially identified by Colin Taylor (letter to the author, 2 December 1991) through a comparison with the Peigan robe noted below (m).

m. Peigan robe collected by Prince Maximilian von Wied in 1833 (Museum für Völkerkunde, Berlin). Illustrated in Krickeberg (1954, pl. 5).

Later Set
The thirteen paintings in the Later Set were executed after settlement on reserves.

a. Painted hide showing Battle of Little Big Horn painted by a Montana Blackfoot around 1876 (Glenbow Museum, Calgary, AF2328).

b. An albino buffalo hide painted by a South Peigan before 1874 (National Museum of the American Indian, Smithsonian Institution, New York, 19/8139).

c. Calf hide depicting the life of Many Shots, a Blood, painted in 1894 (Pitt Rivers Museum, Oxford, 1895.61.1). Illustrated in Maclean 1894.

d. Painted hide inscribed by Red Crane before 1889 (National Museum of the American Indian, Smithsonian Institution, New York, 11/3195). Illustrated (detail) in Grinnell (1896:244).

e. Blackfoot painted hide without documentation (National Museum of the American Indian, Smithsonian Institution, New York, 10/1938).

f. Robe with depictions of Crop Eared Wolf's exploits, Blood, c. 1882 (Royal Canadian Mounted Police Museum, Regina). Illustrated in Barbeau (1960, frontispiece and p. 58).

g. Steer hide painted in 1892 by Sharp, Peigan (National Museum of Natural History, Smithsonian Institution, Washington, D.C., 165,449). Illustrated in Ewers (1983:54).

h. Painted Blackfoot robe, collected 1892–98 (National Museum of Natural History, Smithsonian Institution, Washington, D.C., Cummings Collection, donated 1990).

i. Painted robe, late 19th or early 20th century (Colorado Springs Fine Arts Center, Colorado Springs, TM5567). Illustrated in Colorado Springs Fine Arts Center 1986.

j. Photograph of Seen From Afar's tipi, Blood, 1892 (Glenbow Museum Archives, Calgary, NA-668-7). Illustrated in Dempsey 1980.

k. Painted tipi of Bear Chief, Peigan, c. 1900 (American Museum of Natural History, New York, 323582). Illustrated in Farr (1984:17) and Wissler (1911:38–39).

l. Spotted Calf's tipi, Blackfoot (Siksika), c. 1900; from two photographs (Provincial Archives of Manitoba, Winnipeg, Edmund Morris Collection, 387–88).

m. Painted hide showing the exploits of Wolf Plume, Peigan; said to be 19th century (Glenbow Museum, Calgary, R 676.7). Illustrated in Dempsey (1991:43).

NOTES

1. Although Morris refers to "Butcher" or "Head Chief Butcher," this chief's Blackfoot name is more accurately translated as Leans Over Butchering (Hugh Dempsey, letter to the author, 28 November 1989).

2. When Blackfoot women prepared buffalo skins they first stretched them over the ground by means of pegs. Traditionally the legs, tail, and head, along with the peg holes, were not trimmed from the finished robe, but they were removed from the Morris robes. In addition, there are holes around the outer edges of all five robes, evidently made by a sewing machine, which indicate that the hides were once lined with cloth. These features support the presumption that the Morris robes were at one time used as sleigh or carriage robes.

3. These robes are mentioned in Appendix K of *The Diaries of Nicholas Garry* (Garry 1900:203).

4. Nicolas Point (1967:192) noted with reference to battles occurring in the same "theatre" in which the Blackfoot fought: "Indian fights are very similar to *jeu de barres,* and for this reason last a long time without spilling much blood. Thus, instead of saying, 'We shall fight,' they say, 'We shall have sport.' "

5. "Their principal efforts at pictorial effects, are found on their buffalo robes" (Catlin 1926:278).

6. "While there is time much more is required that has yet to be done by Canada to rescue from oblivion the material for ethnical study in which our vast Dominion is so rich. On all hands we see ancient nations passing away." Morris used this quotation from Daniel Wilson (1883:35) for the frontispiece inscription in the catalogue of his exhibition of Indian portraits and artifacts at the Canadian Art Club in Toronto in 1909 (Morris 1909).

7. This figure does not include the more than fifty artifacts in the Edmund Morris Collection of the Royal Ontario Museum, Toronto, that were acquired by Alexander Morris. Many of these artifacts are of particular importance because the senior Morris collected them during the time he was negotiating treaties in Saskatchewan, Manitoba, and the western tip of Ontario. These are generally older than the Edmund Morris material and have great historic and symbolic significance. Much of the material, including the two shirts presented by Yellow Quill and Sweet Grass, the eagle feather fans, the pipes, and the pipe bags, were gifts of diplomacy and prestige. They were presented by Indian leaders in the same way that medals and military-style jackets were presented by the Dominion of Canada. Included in the four hundred artifacts are some seventy-five Plains items donated to the ROM by Sir Byron Edmund Walker, founding chairman of the Museum. These artifacts are included because they were originally collected in the field by Edmund Morris.

8. This figure includes at least sixty-five named Plains Indian individuals. Morris painted a number of his subjects several times, sometimes working from his own portraits and, perhaps, photographs, other times creating different versions from life.

9. The Edmund Morris diary in the Royal Ontario Museum, Toronto, is a second draft of the years 1907–9, with additional entries covering Morris' 1910 visits to

prairie reserves. Apparently Morris did not keep a diary of his visits in 1911. The Edmund Morris diary in the Provincial Archives of Manitoba, Winnipeg, is a first draft of the years 1907–9; this version of the diary has recently been transcribed (Morris 1993). The ROM has the largest collection of Morris portraits. The remaining extant portraits are fairly widely dispersed: the Government of Saskatchewan, the Provincial Museum of Alberta, Edmonton, and the Peabody Museum of Archeology and Ethnology, Cambridge, Mass., have important holdings.

10. It was quite common for warriors to commission skilled draughtsmen within the tribe to paint their robes. In such cases, however, the warrior who accomplished the deeds would have carefully supervised their painting.

11. George Grinnell was a noted Blackfoot and Cheyenne ethnologist.

12. Edmund Morris to Phimister Proctor, undated letter, Archives of the Art Gallery of Ontario, Toronto, E. J. Stone Donation, Morris File No. 3.

13. The robe of Many Shots is presently in the collection of the Pitt Rivers Museum, Oxford (1895.61.1).

14. Schuster (1987) made a significant contribution to the discussion on the relationship between hide painting and rock art in the Northern Plains.

15. For examples of Blackfoot V-necks, see Appendix, Early Set, a–c, g, m. These V-neck figures also show up in Paul Kane's transposition of his 1845 sketch of the robe of Sinew Piece, a Blood, onto his painting of Big Snake's brother (ROM 912.1.54).

16. There is, however, a shirt in the Civico Museo Lazzar Spallanzani, Reggio Emilia, Italy (no. 113), that bears V-neck figures and is connected with the eastern Sioux (see Colin Taylor *in* Laurencich-Minelli 1990:202). The shirt was collected some time between 1831 and 1844. The robe painted by the Mandan and collected by Lewis and Clark in 1805 also bears a few V-neck figures (Peabody Museum of Archeology and Ethnology, Cambridge, Mass., 99-12-10/53121).

17. For examples of Crow V-necks see Bernisches Historisches Museum, Bern (N.A.4); National Museum of the American Indian, Smithsonian Institution, New York (1/2558, 17/6345); and Nationalmuseet, Copenhagen (Hd.60). See also the drawing of an Hidatsa made by Rudolph Friederich Kurz, 2 August 1851 (Kurz 1937, pl. 8).

18. See especially the Karl Bodmer drawing of a Blackfoot warrior's robe, 30 June 1833 (Thomas and Ronnefeldt 1976:17). The other two shield-bearers are perhaps marginal (Appendix, Early Set, a, l).

19. See Magne and Klassen (1991:414) for a discussion of artistic continuity in the rock art at Writing-On-Stone, Alberta.

20. In 1832 George Catlin painted the portrait of Bull's Back Fat (Hassrick 1981:169). He was fifty years of age and a chief of the Blood tribe at the time.

21. Two other examples of this type are found in the drawings of Rudolph Friederich Kurz and George Catlin. In Kurz's *Journal* there is a figure, drawn in 1851, shown wearing a tabulatory robe (Kurz 1937, pl. 8). Although the only tribe mentioned in association with the several figures in the drawing is Hidatsa, there is some doubt that this attribution would apply to the figure in question, since the Hidatsa system of graded war honours is probably based more on touching the

enemy, i.e., "counting coup," than on capturing weapons. Catlin's drawing shows Buffalo's Child, a Blackfoot, wearing a robe that appears to be of the tabulatory type (Catlin 1926, pl. 17).

22. Compare Wissler 1911:36, Curtis 1911:10, and Ewers 1957:139. For example, while Wissler and Curtis agree that the greatest war honour was to capture a gun from an enemy, Wissler and Ewers were under the impression that the Blackfoot did not credit the formal act of touching an enemy under dangerous circumstances, whereas Curtis suggests that indeed the Blackfoot did give secondary credit for "counting coup."

23. Kurz (1937:154) suggested another possible meaning for object tabulations. In describing the importance of largesse in Plains culture he noted that gifts were so highly accredited that they were sometimes designated on robes as if they were coups.

24. The large number of entrenched battle scenes in the Morris robes reflects the importance of defensive strategies in Blackfoot warfare. J. C. Ewers (letter to the author, 22 February 1993; Ewers 1944:191) has pointed out that this aspect of warfare has been excessively overshadowed in the literature by more sensational, offensive manoeuvres such as counting coup. It should be kept in mind that despite the violence and loss of life portrayed in the war paintings, military success and war honours had meaning only if one's people suffered little loss. For this reason, such defensive stands, whether taking place in natural coulees, war lodges, or quickly excavated fox-holes, are represented in war paintings.

25. A robe in the Department of Anthropology, National Museum of Natural History, Smithsonian Institution, Washington D.C. (2130), is catalogued as from the upper Missouri, c. 1835; it does not appear to be Blackfoot. A robe in the National Museum of the American Indian, Smithsonian Institution, New York (3/2598), is catalogued as Otoe (?), but many features on this robe indicate Blackfoot origins. A robe in the Musée de l'Homme, Paris (86.17.1), catalogued as Mandan and given to the museum in 1804, bears one figure in the lower central portion that may be carrying a war-medicine skin.

26. See Nagy (1991:30) for a discussion on "continuous pictorial narrative" in Plains Indian pictorial painting.

27. The "head and tail" robes were considered of greater value by fur trader and native wearer alike (see Kurz 1937:251; Marquis 1928:62–63).

28. "[Paintings showing] the Act of drawing the Beaver from the Vault and small landscapes with animals [and] Copper Shields or of Tin with Paintings of a frightful animal, red color, will please the Plains Indians" (Garry 1900:201).

29. Nicolas Point collected eleven Indian drawings on paper. One is a "letter" drawn in traditional-style picture-writing and is dated 1842, but has no tribal attribution. The other ten drawings were executed by a Blackfoot in 1846–47. The content of these ten works is not related to warfare but is largely concerned with various aspects of life centring around the trading post. Furthermore, the visual language of these works has many more similarities to European-style painting than to traditional Blackfoot painting. J. C. Ewers (in Point 1967:xi) suggested that these works may have been painted by a Blackfoot protégé of Point.

30. J. C. Ewers (personal communication, 1991) expressed the opinion that before Crop Eared Wolf painted his exploits on the robe (Appendix, Later Set, f)

the "box and border" design was painted by a non-Blackfoot woman.

31. This is not to say that the early paintings were lacking in detail or subtlety. For example, the rendering of knees and calf muscles on an early robe (Appendix, Early Set, a; see Fig. 12) shows sensitive treatment of the human form while not intending to achieve anatomical accuracy.

32. I found the concepts developed by Deregowski and other perceptual psychologists, particularly their notion of eidolic and epitomic images, to be very useful in defining the pictographic style of the Blackfoot.

33. See Lincoln (1992) and Greene (1992:50) for excellent discussions on how Plains Indian pictorial artists responded to changing conditions brought on by the non-native community.

34. Morris collected another drawing on paper bearing the inscription "drawn by 'He Who Tells', an old Assiniboine." It is likely that He Who Tells also painted a set of Assiniboine works on paper, preserved in the Glenbow Museum, Calgary (985.221.130–170).

35. Calf Child was unable to paint his own exploits because of poor eyesight. His son Joe began painting the robe but he proved "too dilatory" and so other draughtsmen were enlisted to complete the task (Morris 1985:102).

36. William Farr noted that the Blackfoot did little to chronicle the early reservation years, but that their oral traditions "continued to reflect an earlier period of buffalo and war, confirming the old patterns, spurning the new" (Farr 1984:188).

37. "Joe [Calf Child's son] makes me a drawing of his father & some other Blackfoot attacked by Crees, his father comes out of the coolies & kills them" (from the diary of Edmund Morris, 1907–9, first draft, p. 16, Provincial Archives of Manitoba, Winnipeg).

38. The medals were from the Duke of York, Lord Minto, and the eminent Chinese statesman Li Hung Chang (Morris 1985:18).

39. Morris Papers. See similar letters from Weasel Calf and Iron Shield that note the cutback of food rations, dated 25 January 1909 and 27 January 1909, respectively (Morris Papers). The moccasins and pipe bag are presently in the Edmund Morris Collection of the Royal Ontario Museum (HK568 and HK566, respectively).

40. Father Léon Doucet to Edmund Morris, 17 March 1909 (Morris Papers).

41. McClintock (1910:427) notes that Running Wolf carried the medal of his father.

42. As spiritual protection on the warpath Running Rabbit wore in his hair an amulet consisting of a round mirror decorated with weasel skins and eagle and magpie feathers. It had formerly been used by his older brother, Many Swans (Hugh A. Dempsey, 1990, manuscript for the entry "Running Rabbit" in the forthcoming new edition of the *Dictionary of Canadian Biography*). Leans Over Butchering owed his success as a warrior to the protective power of the feather-legged hawk which came to him when on a vision quest at the age of seventeen (Schultz 1930:193).

43. Father Léon Doucet to Edmund Morris, 25 August 1908 (Morris Papers).

44. Father Léon Doucet to Edmund Morris, 2 May 1909 (Morris Papers).

45. See letters from Weasel Calf and Iron Shield, dated 25 January 1909 and 27 January 1909, respectively (Morris Papers).

46. The diary of Edmund Morris, 1907–9, first draft, p. 7, Provincial Archives of Manitoba, Winnipeg.

47. Lucien Hanks (Hanks and Hanks 1950:46) noted with reference to the Siksika that opposition to the sale of land "was led by dauntless old warrior chiefs." Samek (1987:111) recorded the same tendency in the sale of Peigan reserve land.

48. Father Léon Doucet to Edmund Morris, 1907–9 (Morris Papers).

49. Father Léon Doucet to Edmund Morris, 2 May 1909 (Morris Papers).

50. Father Léon Doucet to Edmund Morris, 5 June 1909 (Morris Papers).

51. Father Léon Doucet to Edmund Morris, 17 July 1908 (Morris Papers).

52. McClintock (1910:45) also notes that Bull Plume kept a pictographic history of the Peigan. The Glenbow Museum, Calgary, has a pictographic tribal history, or "winter count," painted by Bull Plume, which consists of tiny images drawn in an Indian Department account book (Hugh A. Dempsey, letter to the author, 20 February 1993).

53. Father Léon Doucet to Edmund Morris, 9 December 1908 (Morris Papers).

54. A similar situation occurred in the early 1800s when two Blackfoot chiefs, Painted Feather and Bull's Back Fat, presented the Hudson's Bay Company with their war history robes, presumably to be officially recognized by the HBC as tribal representatives in matters of trade (Garry 1900:203).

55. In 1905 McClintock (1910:415) took note of the rivalry between Bull Plume and Running Wolf: "Bull Plume was a comparatively young man, ambitious for reputation and influence, while the aged Brings-Down-the-Sun [Running Wolf] was universally revered, because of his honesty and kindness of heart, and his life-long reputation for high character and knowledge of sacred ceremonies." When both men were competing for McClintock's attention, Running Wolf, who came from a long line of chiefs, discredited Bull Plume by pointing out that he was still young and had come to live among the Peigan as an orphan.

56. Father Léon Doucet to Edmund Morris, 11 April 1908 (Morris Papers).

57. Father Léon Doucet to Edmund Morris, 17 March 1909 (Morris Papers).

58. Elizabeth Hodgson to Edmund Morris, 3 December 1908 (Morris Papers).

59. Schultz (1930:193–211) devoted almost a full chapter to Leans Over Butchering's account of this exploit. The details regarding the role of supernatural powers in the success of the raiding party are particularly interesting.

60. There are about seven instances in the translations of the Morris robes in which sparing the life of an enemy was credited as a kind of war honour. When Leans Over Butchering was on one of his first war parties his life was spared by an enemy (Hugh A. Dempsey, letter to the author, 20 February 1993). As an old man Leans Over Butchering recounted his coups to

Schultz (1930) and gave special emphasis to two "coups" that were marked by the sparing of life, one out of pity for the enemy, the other out of respect for his enemy's bravery.

61. On 28 October 1911 the Toronto *Globe* published an article on a Sarcee painting: "Two years ago there was a great festival at which seven of the oldest chiefs related the stories of their exploits, which the painter of the tribe preserved for posterity on two immense steer hides" sewn together. The hide is presently in the collection of the Glenbow Museum, Calgary (AF815). Most of the depictions are undoubtedly the work of Two Guns. A number of Bull Head's deeds are represented on the hide and they are briefly translated in the *Globe* article. By comparing the robes of both museums it is apparent that several events on the ROM robe (scenes 3 and 4 and the tabulation of weapons and horses) also appear on the Glenbow robe.

62. It is evident from the Morris robes that Blackfoot warriors treated enemy women as victims and recorded events involving killing or capturing women in context with war exploits. There are at least seven events on the Morris robes that show women as victims. Polygamy was widely accepted among Plains tribes, and captured women generally became wives of their captors. I recently talked with an Assiniboine woman who recalled the seven scars on her mother caused by a Blackfoot raider who, after unsuccessfully trying to convince her to become his wife, attempted to stab her to death (Jessie Saulteux, Carry the Kettle Reserve, interview, November 1992).

63. There are several accounts of the battle involving Father Lacombe, and it is interesting to note the variations and additions contained in the various reports. Two reports come from Cree sources. In 1923 Edward Ahenakew, a Cree writer, recorded an account given by chief Thunderchild (Ahenakew 1973:37), who was present at the battle as a novitiate. Thunderchild's chronicle is distinct from the other accounts in its eloquent description of the tragic and emotional aspects of the battle. The other Cree report was given by Tying Knot and recorded by Edmund Morris (1985:143). Both Cree accounts agree that the raid was mounted in order to avenge the deaths of a group of women (fifteen according to Thunderchild) who were killed by the Blackfoot when they were away from the camp drawing water. The father of two of the women went through all the camps of the Cree, crying for his daughters, and by his grief moved a great number to revenge. As firearms became more widely accessible the Cree discontinued the practice of mounting large vengeance raids because they became too risky. In this instance, the motive for revenge must have been exceptional since both Cree and Blackfoot were well stocked with guns. According to Tying Knot some Cree wanted to kill Lacombe, whereas others would let him go. He goes on to note that the Cree found lots of bibles and crosses which they heaped in a pile and burned. Thunderchild describes how, in the midst of the battle, a Cree put on Lacombe's robe and called out, "Here is the Priest" (Ahenakew 1973:38). Other accounts indicate that the Cree were much more favourably disposed to Lacombe. Morris (1985:125) noted from an unnamed source that "after a time the priest made himself heard, & the Crees retreated for they were attached to Father Lacombe and had they known he was in camp, would never have attacked." Morris further noted: "The Crees took his prayer book & other things but, when they knew of the owner, returned them." Hugh A. Dempsey (1972:49) also wrote an account of the battle, largely based on writings of Father Lacombe. In comparing the accounts of Thunderchild, Tying Knot, Calf Child, the unnamed source in Morris, and Lacombe, there are several other discrepancies, including the number of casualties and the role played by the Blackfoot chief Crowfoot.

64. Paul Raczka, personal communication, February 1993.

65. Jo Ann Yellow Horn, Oldman River Cultural Centre, Brocket, Alberta, letter to the author, 20 February 1993.

66. Rose Crowshoe, personal communication, February 1993.

67. McClintock (1933a, 1933b) recorded several Blackfoot legends given to him by Bull Plume in 1903.

68. Father Léon Doucet to Edmund Morris, 23 February 1909 (Morris Papers).

69. The information on this early war experience was given to Hugh A. Dempsey by South Peigan in Montana and a North Peigan in Brocket, Alberta (Hugh A. Dempsey, letter to the author, 20 February 1993).

70. Jo Ann Yellow Horn, Oldman River Cultural Centre, Brocket, Alberta, letter to the author, 20 February 1993.

71. Hugh A. Dempsey, 1990, manuscript for the entry "Running Rabbit" in the forthcoming new edition of the *Dictionary of Canadian Biography*. Father Levern in a letter to Edmund Morris, 6 January 1908 (Morris Papers), is somewhat at variance when he notes that Running Rabbit was made a minor chief at the age of twenty on account of his bravery.

72. Hugh A. Dempsey, 1990, manuscript for the entry "Running Rabbit" in the forthcoming new edition of the *Dictionary of Canadian Biography*.

73. Hugh A. Dempsey, 1992, manuscript for the entry "Bull Head" in the forthcoming new edition of the *Dictionary of Canadian Biography*.

74. Hugh A. Dempsey, 1992, manuscript for the entry "Bull Head" in the forthcoming new edition of the *Dictionary of Canadian Biography*.

75. Hugh A. Dempsey, 1992, manuscript for the entry "Bull Head" in the forthcoming new edition of the *Dictionary of Canadian Biography*.

76. See the diary of Edmund Morris, 1907–9, first draft, p. 76, Provincial Archives of Manitoba, Winnipeg.

BIBLIOGRAPHY

Ahenakew, Edward
1973 *Voices of the Plains Cree.* Toronto: McClelland and Stewart.

Barbeau, Marius
1960 *Indian Days on the Western Prairies.* Bulletin no. 163. Anthropological series no. 46. Ottawa: National Museums of Canada. Reprint 1970.

Barry, Patricia S.
1991 *Mystical Themes in Milk River Rock Art.* Edmonton: University of Alberta Press.

Bodmer, Karl. *See* Thomas and Ronnefeldt 1976.

Boyle, David
1904 "Picture Writing." *Annual Archaeological Report 1904.* Appendix to the Report of the Minister of Education, Ontario, pp. 54–57. Toronto: Warwick Bros. and Rutter, 1905.

Brasser, Ted J.
1978 *Tipi Paintings, Blackfoot Style.* National Museum of Man, Mercury Series, Canadian Ethnological Service, Paper no. 43. Ottawa: National Museum of Man.

Brunius, Staffan
1990 "North American Indian Collections at the Folkens Museum-Etnografiska, Stockholm." *European Review of Native American Studies* 4(1):29–34.

Catlin, George
1851 *Illustrations of the Manners, Customs and Condition of the North American Indians.* 2 vols. 8th edition. London: H. G. Bohn. [First published by the author in London, 1841]

1876 *Illustrations of the Manners, Customs and Condition of the North American Indians: With Letters and Notes, Written During Eight Years Travel and Adventure Among the Wildest and Most Remarkable Tribes Now Existing.* 2 vols. London: Chatto and Windus. [First published by the author in London, 1841]

1926 *The North American Indians: Being Letters and Notes on Their Manners, Customs and Conditions, Written During Eight Years Travel Amongst the Wildest Tribes of the Indians in North America, 1832–1839.* 2 vols. Edinburgh: John Grant. [First published by the author in London, 1841, as *Letters and Notes on the Manners, Customs, and Condition of the North American Indians: Written During Eight Years' Travel Amongst the Wildest Tribes of Indians in North America, in 1832, 33, 34, 35, 36, 37, 38, and 39*]

Colorado Springs Fine Arts Center
1986 *Colorado Springs Fine Arts Center: A History and Selections from the Permanent Collections.* Colorado Springs, Colo.: The Center.

Conner, Stuart W., and Betty Lu Conner
1971 *Rock Art of the Montana High Plains.* Exhibition catalogue. Santa Barbara: The Art Galleries, University of California.

Curtis, Edward S.
1909 *Apsaroke Hidatsa.* Vol. 4 of *The North American Indian.* Cambridge, Mass.: The University Press.

1911 *Piegan Cheyenne Arapaho.* Vol. 6 of *The North American Indian.* Norwood, Mass.: The Plimpton Press.

Dempsey, Hugh A.
1968 *Blackfoot Ghost Dance.* Glenbow Museum Occasional Paper no. 3. Calgary. Reprinted 1982.

1972 *Crowfoot: Chief of the Blackfeet.* Edmonton: Hurtig.

1980 *Red Crow: Warrior Chief.* Saskatoon: Western Producer Prairie Books.

1991 *Treasures of the Glenbow Museum.* Calgary: Glenbow Museum.

Dempsey, James
1988 "Persistence of a Warrior Ethic Among the Plains Indians." *Alberta History* 36(1):1–10.

Deregowski, Jan B.
1980 *Illusions, Patterns, and Pictures: A Cross-Cultural Perspective.* London/Boston: Academic Press.

1984 *Distortion in Art: The Eye and the Mind.* London/Boston: Routledge and Kegan Paul.

Dunn, Dorothy
1968 *American Indian Painting of the Southwest and Plains Areas.* Albuquerque: University of New Mexico.

Eng, Helga K.
1931 *The Psychology of Children's Drawings from First Stroke to the Coloured Drawing.* London: K. Paul, Trench Trubner.

Ewers, John Canfield
1939 *Plains Indian Painting: A Description of an Aboriginal American Art.* Stanford University and London: Stanford University Press and Oxford University Press.

1944 "The Blackfoot War Lodge: Its Construction and Use." *American Anthropologist* 46:182–92.

1945 *Blackfeet Crafts.* Laurence, Kansas: United States Indian Service.

1957 *Early White Influence Upon Plains Indian Painting: George Catlin and Carl Bodmer Among the Mandan, 1832–34.* Smithsonian Miscellaneous Collections, vol. 134, no. 7. Washington, D.C.: Smithsonian Institution.

1958 *The Blackfeet: Raiders on the Northwestern Plains.* Civilization of the American Indian Series, no. 49. Norman: University of Oklahoma Press.

1968 "Plains Indian Painting: The History and Development of an American Art Form." *The American West* 5(2):4–15.

1981 "Water Monsters in Plains Indian Art." *American Indian Art Magazine* 6(4):38–45.

1983 "A Century and a Half of Blackfoot Picture Writing." *American Indian Art Magazine* 8(3):52–61.

Farr, William E.
1984 *The Reservation Blackfoot, 1882–1945: A Photographic History of Cultural Survival.* Seattle: University of Washington Press.

Fitz-Gibbon, Mary. *See* Morris 1985.

Fortes, Meyer
1940 "Children's Drawings Among the Tallensi." *Africa* 13:293–95.

Garry, Nicholas
1900 *The Diary of Nicholas Garry, Deputy-Governor of the Hudson's Bay Company: A Detailed Narrative of His Travels in the Northwest Territories.* Royal Society of Canada, Proceedings and Transactions, Second Series, vol. 6, Transactions, Section 2, pp. 73–204. Montreal: Gazette Printing Co.

Glenbow-Alberta Institute
1987 *The Spirit Sings: Artistic Traditions of Canada's First Peoples: A Catalogue of the Exhibition.* Toronto/Calgary: McClelland and Stewart/The Glenbow Museum.

Goldfrank, Esther Schiff
1945 *Changing Configurations in the Social Organization of a Blackfoot Tribe During the Reserve Period (The Blood of Alberta, Canada).* American Ethnological Society, Monograph 8. New York: J. J. Augustin.

Greene, Candace S.
1992 "Artists in Blue: The Indian Scouts of Fort Reno and Fort Supply." *American Indian Art Magazine* 18(1):50–57.

Grinnell, George Bird
1892 *Blackfoot Lodge Tales: The Story of a Prairie People.* New York: Scribner and Sons.

1896 *The Story of the Indians.* New York: D. Appleton and Co.

1910 "Coup and Scalp Among the Plains Indians." *American Anthropologist,* n.s. 12:296–310.

Hall, H. U.
1926 "A Buffalo Robe Biography." *The Museum Journal* 17(1):5–37. Philadelphia: The University Museum of the University of Pennsylvania.

Hanks, Lucien M., Jr., and Jane Richardson Hanks
1950 *Tribe under Trust: A Study of the Blackfoot Reserve of Alberta*. Toronto: University of Toronto Press.

Harper, J. Russell
1971 *Paul Kane's Frontier*. Toronto: University of Toronto Press.

Hassrick, Royal B.
1981 *The George Catlin Book of American Indians*. New York: Promontory Press.

Hoffman, Walter J.
1895 *The Beginnings of Writing*. New York: D. Appleton and Co.

Howard, James H.
1954 "Plains Indian Feather Bonnets." *Plains Anthropologist* 2:24–27.

Kane, Paul
1858 *Wanderings of an Artist Among the Indians of North America*. London: Spottiswoode and Co.

Keyser, James D.
1977 "Writing-On-Stone: Rock Art of the Northwestern Plains." *Canadian Journal of Archaeology* 1:15–80.

Kidd, Kenneth E.
1986 *Blackfoot Ethnography*. Archaeological Survey of Alberta, Manuscript Series, no. 8. Edmonton: Alberta Culture, Historical Resources Division.

Krickeberg, Walter
1954 *Ältere Ethnographica aus Nordamerika im Berliner Museum für Völkerkunde*. D. Reiner: Berlin.

Kurz, Rudolph Friederich
1937 *Journal of Rudolph Friederich Kurz: An Account of His Experiences Among Fur Traders and American Indians on the Mississippi and the Upper Missouri Rivers During the Years 1846 to 1852*. Smithsonian Institution, Bureau of American Ethnology, Bulletin 115. Washington, D.C.: United States Printing Office.

Laurencich-Minelli, Laura
1990 "Antonio Spagni and His Collection in Reggio Emilia." *Plains Anthropologist* 35(128):191–204.

Lewis, Oscar
1942 *The Effects of White Contact upon Blackfoot Culture*. American Ethnological Society, Monograph 6. New York: J. J. Augustin.

Lincoln, Louise
1992 "The Social Construction of Plains Indian Art." In *Visions of the People: A Pictorial History of Plains Indian Life*, by Evan M. Maurer, pp. 47–59. Minneapolis: Minneapolis Institute of Arts.

Loendorf, Laurence L.
1990 "A Dated Rock Art Panel of Shield Bearing Warriors in South Central Montana." *Plains Anthropologist* 35(127):45–54.

Maclean, John
1894 "Picture Writing of the Blackfeet." *Canadian Institute Transactions* 5:114–18; plates in *Canadian Institute Transactions*, supplement to no. 9, vol. 5, part 1.

1896 *Canadian Savage Folk: The Native Tribes of Canada*. Toronto: William Briggs.

Magne, Martin P. R., and Michael A. Klassen
1991 "A Multivariate Study of Rock Art Anthropomorphs at Writing-On-Stone, Southern Alberta." *American Antiquity* 56(3):389–418.

Mallery, Garrick
1889 *Picture Writing of the American Indians*. Bureau of American Ethnology. Reprinted with a foreword by J. W. Powell. New York: Dover Publications, 1972.

Marquis, Thomas B., ed.
1928 *Memories of a White Crow Indian*. New York: Century.

Maurer, Evan M.
1992 *Visions of the People: A Pictorial History of Plains Indian Life*. Minneapolis: Minneapolis Institute of Arts.

McClintock, Walter
1910 *The Old North Trail*. London: MacMillan and Co.

1933a "The Twin Brothers." *The Masterkey* 7(2):41–46. Los Angeles: Southwest Museum.

1933b "The Story of Belly Fat." *The Masterkey* 11(3):70–73. Los Angeles: Southwest Museum.

1936 *Painted Tipis and Picture Writing of the Blackfoot Indians.* Southwest Museum Leaflet no. 6. Los Angeles: Southwest Museum.

McGinnis, Anthony R.
1974 "Intertribal Conflict on the Northern Plains, 1738–1889." Ph.D. diss. University of Colorado. Ann Arbor: Xerox University Microfilms.

Miller, Judi; Elizabeth Moffatt; and Jane Sirois
1990 "Native Materials Project: Final Report. November 1990." Ottawa: Canadian Conservation Institute.

Mishkin, Bernard
1940 *Rank and Warfare Among the Plains Indians.* American Ethnological Society, Monograph 3. Seattle: University of Washington Press.

Morris, Edmund Montague
1909 *Canadian Art Club Exhibition of Indian Portraits with Notes on the Tribes by Edmund Morris, Together with Loan Collections of Objects of Indian Art and Curios. . . .* Toronto: Canadian Art Club, Miln-Bingham, Printers.

1985 *The Diaries of Edmund Montague Morris: Western Journeys 1907–1910.* Transcribed by Mary Fitz-Gibbon. Toronto: Royal Ontario Museum.

1993 *Edmund M. Morris: A Transcription of His Journal: 1907–1909 Western Journeys.* Transcribed by John S. R. O'Malley. Winnipeg: John S. R. O'Malley. [Self-published]

Morris Papers
Morris, Edmund Montague. Archival Papers. Provincial Archives of Manitoba, Winnipeg, MG14C30.

Nagy, Imre
1991 "Progress or Decline? White Impact on the Pictographic Art of the Plains Indians." *European Review of Native American Studies* 5(1):29–33.

O'Malley, John S. R. *See* Morris 1993.

Petersen, Karen Daniels
1971 *Plains Indian Art from Fort Marion.* Civilization of the American Indian Series, vol. 101. Norman: University of Oklahoma Press.

Point, Nicolas
1967 *Wilderness Kingdom: Indian Life in the Rocky Mountains: 1840–1847: The Journals and Paintings of Nicolas Point.* Translated with an introduction by Joseph P. Donnelly, appreciation by John C. Ewers. New York: Holt, Rinehart and Winston.

Raczka, Paul M.
1992 "Sacred Robes of the Blackfoot and Other Northern Plains Tribes." *American Indian Art Magazine* 17(3):66–73.

Reuning, H., and Wendy Wortley
1973 *Psychological Studies of the Bushmen.* Johannesburg: National Institute for Personnel Research.

Rodee, Howard D.
1965 "The Stylistic Developments of Plains Indian Painting and Its Relationship to Ledger Drawings." *Plains Anthropologist* 10(30):218–32.

Samek, Hana
1987 *The Blackfoot Confederacy, 1880–1920: A Comparative Study of Canadian and U.S. Indian Policy.* Albuquerque: University of New Mexico Press.

Schultz, James Willard, and Jessie Louise Donaldson
1930 *The Sun God's Children.* Cambridge, Mass.: The Riverside Press.

Schuster, Helen H.
1987 "Tribal Identification of Wyoming Rock Art: Some Problematic Considerations." *Archaeology in Montana* 28(2):25–43.

Smith, Marian W.
1938 "The War Complex of the Plains Indians." *Proceedings of the American Philosophical Society* 78(3):425–64.

Stocken, Canon H. W. Gibbon
1976 *Among the Blackfeet and Sarcee.* Calgary: Glenbow-Alberta Institute.

Taylor, Colin
1986 "Catlin's Portrait of Iron Horn: An Early Style of Blackfeet Shirt." *Plains Anthropologist* 31(114), part 1, pp. 265–79.

Thomas, Davis, and Karin Ronnefeldt, eds.
1976 *People of the First Man: Life Among the Plains Indians in Their Final Days of Glory: The Firsthand Account of Prince Maximilian's Expedition up the Missouri River, 1833–34.* Watercolors by Karl Bodmer. New York: E. P. Dutton.

Vatter, Ernst
1927 "Historienmalerei und heraldische Bilderschrift der Nordamerikanischen Präriestämme: Beiträge zu einer ethnographischen und stilistischen Analyse" ("History Paintings and Heraldic Pictographs of the North American Indians: A Contribution Towards the Ethnographic and Stylistic Analysis"). In *IPEK: Jahrbuch für prähistorische & ethnographische Kunst (Annual Review of Prehistoric and Ethnographical Art)*, edited by Herbert Kühn, pp. 46–81. Leipzig: Klinkhardt and Biermann.

Vitart, Anne, ed.
1993 *Parures d'histoire: Peaux de bisons peintes des Indiens d'Amérique du Nord.* Paris: Musée de l'Homme.

Walton, Ann T; John C. Ewers; and Royal B. Hassrick
1985 *After the Buffalo Were Gone: The Louis Warren Hill, Sr., Collection of Indian Art.* St. Paul, Minn.: Northwest Area Foundation.

Wied, Maximilian, Prinz von. *See* Thomas and Ronnefeldt 1976.

Wilson, Daniel
1883 "Pre-Aryan Man." In *Royal Society of Canada, Proceedings and Transactions, 1882–1883.* Vol. 1, section 2, pp. 35–71. Montreal: Dawson Brothers.

Wissler, Clark
1911 *The Social Life of the Blackfoot Indians.* American Museum of Natural History, Anthropological Papers, vol. 7, part 1, pp. 1–64.

1912 *Social Organization and Ritualistic Ceremonies of the Blackfoot Indians.* American Museum of Natural History, Anthropological Papers, vol. 7, part 2, pp. 65–298.

1913 *Societies and Dance Associations of the Blackfoot Indians.* American Museum of Natural History, Anthropological Papers, vol. 11, part 4, pp. 359–460.

Wolfe, Alexander
1988 *Earth Elder Stories.* Saskatoon: Fifth House.

Young, Gloria A.
1986 "The Visual Language of Plains Indian Ledger Art." In *The Art of the North American Indians: Native Traditions in Evolution,* edited by E. L. Wade, pp. 45–62. Tulsa: Philbrooke Art Center, and New York: Hudson Hills Press.